STILL

WITH

ME

A Daughter's Journey of Love and Loss

ANDREA KING COLLIER

SIMON & SCHUSTER

New York   London   Toronto   Sydney   Singapore

SIMON & SCHUSTER
Rockefeller Center
1230 Avenue of the Americas
New York, New York 10020

SIMON & SCHUSTER
and colophon are registered trademarks
of Simon & Schuster Inc.

For information about special discounts for bulk purchases,
please contact Simon & Schuster Special Sales:
1-800-456-6798 or business@simonandschuster.com

Manufactured in the United States of America

10 9 8 7 6 5 4 3 2 1

Library of Congress Cataloging-in-Publication Data

Collier, Andrea King.
Still with me / Andrea King Collier.
p. cm.
1. Terry, Earline Comer—Health. 2. Ovaries—Cancer—
Patients—Nevada—Biography. I. Title.

RC280.O8 T4542003
362.1'9699465'0092—dc21
[B]   2002026674

ISBN 0-7432-2610-0

This book is dedicated to the spirit and inspiration who drove its writing, Earline Comer Terry.

And to Darnay, Nicole, and Christopher Collier, who walked every step of this story with me.

ACKNOWLEDGMENTS

To my family: Louis and Lucille Comer; Gladys Comer; Robert Comer; Gloria Comer North; Danny, Ronald, and Rhonda North and their children. John Terry, my stepfather, and Bertha King, my stepmother, who is one of the strongest, most loving women I know.

My guardian angels and sweet sister-friends to my mother: Gussie Kaufman, Josephine Good, Katherine Lorden, Imogene Edwards, Hortense Williams, Grace Turner, Frances McDowell, and, of course, Mildred Calloway. And Fay Price, who still reminds me that I have been very loved.

The world's best in-laws, Willie and Jeannie Collier, who took me in, dusted me off, and have made me feel at home for over twenty years.

My warrior woman–diva agent, Wendy Sherman; Andrea Mullins, my original editor; and Ruth Fecych, the wonderful editor who waved me in to home base on this book.

My soul friends, Art Houser, Robert Alexander, Leslie Taylor, Renee Miller, Lisa King, Deb Hollis, Karen Lee, Lydia Holmes, Brenda Morris, Candace Bell, Linda Newbury, and Barb

ACKNOWLEDGMENTS

Mastin, who have always understood. My "from the very beginning" girls, Willette Gee Brown and Angela Butler.

Linda Peckham for her guidance and encouragement when I didn't think I had it in me. Everybody in The Forum for Writers at Lansing Community College, and the LCC Foundation for its support. Chris Henning for being an angel.

My moms and confidantes in the writing life, Pat Rahmann and Rochelle Distellheim and the most fabulous group of writers a girl would ever want to have in her corner, the Writer Chicks—Min Jin, Gina, Anne, Jane St. C, Alicia, Paisley, Pam, Clarice, Leslie, Karen, Debra Leigh, Heidi, Marlene, Ruth, Diane, Briget, Jennifer, Claire, Mary, Sujata, Nadine, Arlene, Laverne, Sandi, and honorary Chick, Ad.

Amy Bacon Volpe for the friendship and the hookup, Jill Stewart and Sharon Latson for the embrace, and Last Acts for the lessons.

INTRODUCTION

This book was written out of love for a remarkable woman, my mother, Earline Comer Terry. It was also written out of fear. It started out as a fellowship proposal to the Kaiser Foundation for a media journalism fellowship. I wanted to write about hereditary cancers and their effects on family members who heard the ticking time bomb. I had learned all about living with the time bomb ten years ago.

The proposal was declined and I moved on to other writing projects. Yet I had a nagging feeling that there was more to this story than my screaming DNA. Over the next few months I'd jot down notes about the year that my mother was ill. I pulled out the journals that I hadn't wanted to look at for ten years and suddenly found myself telling a story because she wanted me to tell it.

I had always looked for something positive to draw out of our experience, yet most days it was impossible to find the "good" in it. But once I figured out that I wasn't the only one, and that many more daughters would walk down the same path with their own mothers, I knew I needed to share my experiences and to talk about what I learned in the process.

INTRODUCTION

On one level, this is a book about health and the lack of it. It's also about hope and fighting cancer and the fear of inheriting it and passing it on to another generation. It is also simply a story of two women, a mother and a daughter, who loved each other more than any words in this book could ever say.

ONE

"The doctors here say they think I have some kind of cancer," my mother said on the phone, from Las Vegas.

It was on July 25, 1992, my ninth wedding anniversary.

I don't remember hearing anything else. When your mother calls and says that she has cancer, all of the air flies out of the room, out of your lungs, out of your gut, out of your heart. You can't breathe and you can't hear.

If she had said that the doctors thought she had just a touch of cancer, like a touch of the flu, I might have been able to catch my breath. All I wanted to hear were the words that would make it all better. Throughout my whole life, she'd been the one person who could fix anything no matter how messy or hopeless. If she had said that her cancer was less than stage one (which is the best stage to have, if you have to have cancer), I'd have heard that. She could have told me that there would be no need for surgery, or chemotherapy. I know I would have heard her loud and clear if she had told me that it was just a small thing and that the doctors in Las Vegas were sure she would have a complete and quick recovery.

I needed her to patch this up, add one more piece of information that would take the hurt off the words "The doctors here say they think I have some kind of cancer." Then I could hear. Then I could breathe again.

But she didn't say any of that. She just sighed, long and slow and deep, and that said everything about what she was feeling. There was so much fear and pain in her sigh that it made me sigh too. There was no weeping or wailing for us, but we each cried silently. Across the phone lines I could see her large, round brown eyes brimming with tears, and I knew that somehow she could see my face too.

In an odd way, I felt a little relieved. Two weeks before, she had visited my family for a week, and we'd been shocked by how thin and sick she looked. I now had an explanation.

When my mother had announced that she was coming for a visit, just after I'd lost a job offer, I figured I was destined to be out of work to get ready for her arrival. I went through the house like an obsessive-compulsive maniac. I dusted things that normally never got dusted. I rearranged pictures along the fireplace mantel, replacing one of my father, stepmother, half brother, and me with a black-and-white portrait of me as a baby, dressed in a fluffy little dress and lacy socks, perched on my mother's lap. You could tell by the pose that she was telling me to look at the camera and smile pretty for Mommy.

I spit-shined our kids, Christopher and Nicole, and begged them to stay clean, at least until I could pick up Granny from the airport, although I knew it would be hard for a two-year-old boy and a six-year-old girl to do. She'd kiss and hug all the stuffing out of them, but would also inspect them from head to toe, making sure that we were not starving them, depriving them, or dressing them like ragamuffins.

My mothering skills were on the line, but I knew she would judge me more by how the children looked and smelled than whether or not they threw food or said please and thank you.

When I was growing up, she was a strict disciplinarian. But she had clearly outgrown it. Now, a grandchild having a full-court, screaming fit about a plaything in Toys "R" Us, turned out to be much more acceptable to my mother than chocolate ice cream on his T-shirt (which would end up being my fault anyway).

Her only expectation now was that I keep them clean and cute. All other little-thug behavior was acceptable. Go figure.

After feeling confident that I had isolated the children from any mess, and felt semi sure that they would be clean when I got back, I moved on to the kitchen, giving it a light going over, again, and again, and again. Then I vacuumed the dining room rug for the fourth time.

I second-guessed everything, trying to hide all my house-keeping warts. I needed to be a big girl who met with her approval. I had to show her I could run a house and manage a family.

"God, when will this visit be over?" I said, thinking I was alone.

"You're already acting crazy as hell, and she hasn't even gotten off the plane yet," my husband, Darnay, reminded me. "Relax." Easy for him to say.

He had no idea. When your mother comes to visit, your meat loaf recipe is never right. Your cakes always fall. You're self-conscious about using mayo instead of Miracle Whip, which, she will remind you, "has been used by women in our family for years."

Before you know it, you spin so far out of control that you don't quite fit comfortably in the skin you wore like a champ just a day ago. In my case, I had gone from being a strong woman who made giant decisions about business and clients and dinner and children every day, a woman whom other people called for advice, to a little girl who needed to please her mommy.

I was late getting to the airport but the plane was too. I paced, using the time to rehearse good answers to all the questions I knew she would ask. *Yes, I have more things to wear than baggy sweatpants and baseball caps. No, I don't think my haircut is too short. No, I'm not worried that if I dress that way out in public, people will think I'm gay. No, we don't have a couch yet. No, thank you, we want to buy it ourselves.*

When her plane finally came in, I walked right past her. I was looking for the mother I had seen six months before. She wore a size twelve, sometimes a fourteen. She normally would have had on one of those swishy jogging suits in pastel colors. She loved them. "They make you look neat when you travel," she'd say. She'd be carefully made up, following the ironclad rule of women in my clan, which was to never leave the house without your lipstick on.

She'd have on a brown, reddish brown, or sandy brown short, but fluffy, wig—whatever was catching her fancy. And she'd have a big, wide smile. "Baby," she'd say.

I watched and waited while people filed off the plane and hugged their loved ones, but I didn't see her anywhere. I was about to call Vegas to see if she had missed the plane when I spotted the one unclaimed passenger. It was Mother. I recognized the suit, but she was about a size six and it flapped on her like a sheet in the breeze.

Everything about her seemed washed out and gray. Her skin was ashen and her hair was a frizzy mat of tight curls, eight shades of gray that fit on her head like a steel-wool scrubbing pad. As she walked toward me, she moved on tippy toes, tenderly, like her bones hurt, but she smiled with pride, as if her new appearance was perfectly normal.

"See how good I've been doing watching my diet," she said, extending her arms so I could get a good look before she hugged me. I didn't know what to say. I wondered if she had developed some eating disorder since her move from Indiana to Las Vegas.

"That's some diet, all right," was the best, most politic answer I could muster.

So we both pretended that everything was okay. Throughout her visit we all acted as if she looked just as she had the last time we had seen her. We never mentioned the fact that she spent most of her time lying around, watching talk shows and soaps.

I couldn't even enjoy the fact that for the whole two weeks she was there she didn't complain about my clothes or tell me to put on some mascara. She got smaller and smaller by the day, always pushing her food from one side of her plate to the other. Anorexia? When I asked her why she wasn't eating, she never answered.

Nicole showed me that Mother threw the food away, or hid it under discarded newspapers and coffee filters.

"Doesn't Granny like your cooking?" she asked. "She waits until you leave the room, then she scrapes her plate. See?"

At night, when everyone was in bed, Darnay and I weighed whether we should say anything.

"Ask her if she's feeling okay," I told him.

"No way. She's your mother, you ask her," he said. "I don't want her pissed off at me."

Neither of us knew how to ask. What do you say? "You look awful. Las Vegas doesn't agree with you at all. You look like you could use a good pork chop."

There have been times in my life when I would have loved to take a potshot at her (all of middle and high school). But it was clear that something wasn't right. "Maybe she's just tired," I said.

Three days before she flew back home, she rented a little

blue car to drive the three hours to our hometown of Gary, Indiana, to see her father, sister, brother, and some old friends. She'd never lived anywhere but Gary until she was fifty-nine years old. Everybody knew everybody there. Her best friends were the people she had played with even before kindergarten. My childhood friends were the children of her childhood friends. And they were the children of my grandparents' childhood friends. The hardest part of her move to Las Vegas six months before with my stepfather, John, had been leaving the people she had known all her life.

She was so excited about seeing everyone, eating at her favorite place, and shopping at her favorite spots. I was hoping that she'd come back looking a lot better. Maybe going home would give her new energy. Las Vegas had probably been a bad move and she was too proud to admit that she wanted to come home. I wanted to believe that she was simply depressed. We could fix that.

I was also hopeful that at least one of her longtime friends would get Mother to confide in her. There was always the hope that my eighty-six-year-old grandfather and his girlfriend, Ruby, would take one good look at her and tell her that she was looking a little peaked.

Months later, Gussie, the friend she'd stayed with during her visit, told me how concerned she had been. Like me, she hadn't known what to say. "I started to call you but . . ."

She told me that after my mother had gotten there, she'd pretty much stayed in her pajamas. She called people, but told them that she was in Lansing, apparently having decided that she didn't want anyone to know she was in town. The only person she saw was Grandpa, and that was because he was legally blind from glaucoma and cataracts, and could only make out shadows. She timed her visit for when she knew Ruby wouldn't be there. No witnesses.

"I just don't feel like being bothered," she told her friend. But when she got back, she told us that she had flitted around seeing everyone, and they were all so surprised by how well her new life was agreeing with her. "They said I looked better and happier than I have in years," she said.

It would have been my moment to say something, but again I choked. I look back on it now and wonder what would have changed if I had said, "You don't look well." Instead we all acted out "The Emperor's New Clothes."

I almost spoke up on the day she left. The kids had gotten used to having her around, plying them with sweets, buying them whatever they wanted, and giving them all of her attention. They were upset to see her packing.

"Make Granny stay," my daughter said. This made my mother cry, which made me cry too. Seeing me cry made both the kids wail. "You don't have to go, you know," I said. "You could stay. You could stay with us and not go back."

I told her that nobody cared if the move was a mistake. She wasn't the first person to sell her house to move to something better, only to realize that it wasn't better after all. "Las Vegas is not making you happy."

"But John loves Vegas." She looked away, pulling herself together to finish packing. We didn't talk about it again.

At the airport, she insisted that we say good-bye at the curb. "I'll be okay. I'll check my bags here." She nodded to the airport attendant.

Christopher was asleep in his car seat, but Nicole was determined to make sure that Granny got to the gate.

"Nicole," Mother said, "Granny will be so upset to have to say good-bye at the gate. So you would be helping me a lot if you let me kiss you and hug you here. I'll send you and Chris some toys from Circus Circus when I get home."

I unloaded her bags at the curbside check-in and we all

hugged good-bye. When she turned to walk through the automatic doors, I had this quiver of a feeling that it could be the last time I would see her.

It felt like the end, but I couldn't figure out why. I just knew I had made a terrible mistake in letting her go. I should have kept her here. I could have insisted.

After she left, I called John. "What the hell happened to her?" I said. I don't even think I said hello first.

"She doesn't look so good," he said. "I told her she ought to go to the doctor."

But I wanted to know what had happened. A person doesn't wake up one morning and age twenty years without someone asking why. You don't lose three dress sizes in a week and not have your husband notice. "Do you look at her at all? She looks like hell," I said, my voice getting higher and louder with each syllable.

The truth was, he probably hadn't paid her much attention, or her to him, in several years. She must have mentioned him only twice during her whole visit. I wasn't completely convinced that her melancholy wasn't tied to the fact that she'd finally figured out, after all these years, that he was boring. This may not have been an issue before, when she lived in Gary and had her old friends and family to distract her from the fact that the two of them had nothing in common. In Las Vegas, their only diversion was the excitement of the Strip.

I waited to hear more from him about when he'd first figured out that she was sick. But he had no more answers. He hadn't really thought about it. He just knew what he knew: "She doesn't look so good."

TWO

Two days later, John called and asked me if I had heard from her. She'd disappeared. She had gone shopping two days before, but had never come back. "She's gone. Her car is gone. But all her stuff is here."

"Why are you just now calling me?" I was hysterical.

"When she came back, she kept talking about how she hated it here now. She kept talking about how she should come back to you," he said. "So I figured she did." Then he wasn't so sure. "After a couple of days, I got a little worried." *A little worried.*

I grilled him about calling the police and checking the hospitals. He said he would as soon as we got off the phone. I paced, moving from the living room to the kitchen, down the hall, passing through the breakfast room to the dining room, sitting for a minute, then jumping up to go to the living room and starting all over again. I was plotting travel plans. I was going to go look for her, and when I found her, I would bring her to live with me.

About fifteen minutes later, the phone rang again. I jumped to pick it up and heard her shaky, watery voice on the other end saying, "The doctors here say they think I have some kind of cancer." I was so stunned that I didn't even ask her where she had been. The next day she told me that she had started to hemorrhage while out shopping. "I called John to come and get me and I couldn't find him. So I had to drive myself to the hospital." She said she hadn't called him because she was furious that he had not been there when she needed him.

"It's like living by yourself," she said.

"I was scared to death, Ma. How come you didn't at least call?"

She explained that she'd never thought he would call me. "I figured I'd find out what was wrong, get out of the hospital, and call you before you called me. I didn't think it was anything bad. I didn't want you to worry," she said.

Her words "The doctors here say they think I have some kind of cancer," bounced around in my head as whispers, shouts, cries, sighs. My husband had been at work all day planning our anniversary celebration, getting a sitter for the kids and a room with a Jacuzzi, chilled champagne, and roses, but now I couldn't even think about celebrating.

Instead I'm at some somber amusement park in my mind, Six Flags Over Oh Shit, giving the greasy, pimply-faced attendant with the stubby hands my ticket to get on the biggest, scariest, ricketiest wooden roller coaster on earth.

There's a click that lets me know that I'm locked in the seat. Nobody is going to cut me a break. Nobody is going to let me out. Of course, there's really no pimply-faced attendant. There's no one to plead with. Nobody cares that I would rather be making out with my husband because it's our anniversary. Nobody gives a damn that I'd rather be a few feet over, on the mother-daughter-relationship bumper cars, but that's not real. The cancer is real.

*On this day, due to the luck of the draw, I get to move to the front of
the line and ride the "your mother has cancer roller coaster" and I can't
get off. So I hunker down, because it's all I can do. That's all any of us
can do when we get that call. I take a deep breath and tell myself that it
will be okay. Then I feel the next click, and that hard, unexpected jerk
that lurches me forward and drops my stomach to my knees. The ride is
about to start. All I can say is, "Here we go."*

Suddenly I understood why I hadn't gotten that job. I had
big work to do. I stayed up all night, making all the decisions
that needed to be made by seven o'clock the next morning. I
called her three hours later.

"You're moving here," I told her. "I'll look at apartments all
day today."

I rattled off endless questions from the list I'd made in a
thick spiral-bound notebook that I'd labeled "Command
Central." We talked about getting her car to Lansing, and
putting things in storage until her new apartment was ready.
"Fireplace? Two bedrooms?" I'd found the names of the top
oncologists in the area, and as soon as we hung up, I set up
referrals. "Do you prefer a male or a female doctor?" I asked.

We talked for twenty minutes, and all she said was, "Okay."
Then she said, "Slow down, Baby. We don't know. This could be
a long and horrible thing."

"Well, if that's so, we need to be together to fight it. I need
to take care of you. Darnay and your grandkids need to take care
of you." Darnay and I had gone over the pros and cons of the
solution I was recommending, but knew that no matter how
much stress it might cause, it was the right thing to do.

I did need to take care of her. Out of sheer will, I would
make her better. I was sure I knew how.

"My babies," she said. Any objection had melted. Everything
she needed to hear was said. We wanted her. "Well, I have to convince John," she said.

"He's welcome too," I said, loudly sucking on my teeth, not caring. He wasn't my concern. It didn't matter to me if he moved or stayed. My mission was to get my mother well and I had no intention of letting anybody or anything get in the way. "I'll leave that up to you to handle," I told her. "But you're moving here."

During the conversation there were clear cues that she was going to leave the convincing to me. She knew that I simply wouldn't take no for an answer, and that if push came to shove, she couldn't say no to me. If she had to leave him behind, it wouldn't be her fault. That was her leverage.

Later that day, on the phone with my stepfather, I became a world-class diplomat on her behalf. Just a day before, I had screamed at him, accusing him of neglect, stopping just short of calling him an idiot. Now I was in a spot where I had to be as sweet as key lime pie and it reopened old wounds.

She had never married my biological father. I'd seen him only occasionally throughout my childhood. She felt as if she had cheated me out of having a real father. I was twelve when she married John. She probably dated other people, but I never saw them. He was the first one she brought around, so it always seemed to me that she had married the first thing that came along.

When they got married they took me out of the house I had always known, from the grandparents who had helped raise me, away from my friends, and into another house with another dynamic. That first year was awful for everyone. He was determined to be THE DADDY, setting new rules. I was determined that he would not.

"Things are going to be a lot different now, missy," he said, the first day that he had to be alone with me. That was a bad thing to say.

I said awful things to him too. "If you think you're going to change me, you can kiss my butt," I said. "I have a grandma and a grandpa. I have a mother. I have a family, and you are not a part of it." We went at it for hours.

"I won't stay here with you. You're crazy and you are mistreating me," I said. I called my grandfather to come pick me up. He knew that if I left, and if my mother came home to find that he had run me out of the house, it would be curtains for him. As it was, he would never have a good relationship with the in-laws who felt that the sun rose and set on my little face.

My mother got home to find me gone. My grandparents told her what I had carefully crafted to tell them. "This child is hysterical. She's absolutely beside herself. She's having one of her headaches," my grandmother said. Everybody knew that I was prone to exaggerated drama, but it didn't seem to matter.

Twenty minutes later, my mother and John pulled up at my grandparents' house. John had to do all the talking. He made lots of apologies to my grandparents, my mother, and me. He had tears in his eyes. I could only imagine what the whip-tongued Earline had whispered in his ear before they'd gotten there.

At my grandparents' kitchen table, a truce was made that would last the rest of my childhood. He and I said very few words to each other over the next eight years, at best exchanging polite grunting. For the most part, I ignored him. He was clearly scared of me and what I was capable of if I decided that he had to go, so he kept his distance.

This truce had lasted nearly twenty years, until the day he'd called and said that she had disappeared for two days. My throat was scratchy from yelling at him about police and hospitals and missing persons' reports. But I knew I had to soften if I was going to get my mother back where I could take care of her.

"John, we'd love to have you both come here. Our home is your home," I said, sounding like the children's librarian at story hour. The only thing missing was milk and cookies and a nap blankie.

"It will be so hard on you to get through the surgery, the chemo, and whatever lies ahead—alone." It occurred to me that I was talking to him as if he was the one who had cancer.

"Let us help you. Please." He played hard to get, then reluctantly agreed. I had done what she wanted me to and sounded the way she needed me to sound to get what she needed to survive. And he got what he'd always wanted, which was for me to say, "Please, pretty please." It was like eating living, crawling bugs, but it worked.

I was astounded by how quickly the world could morph into something else. Exactly five days later, I was signing a lease on a two-bedroom apartment with a fireplace, a patio, and a man-made duck pond, ten minutes from my house. That same day my mother got on a plane back to Lansing with her medical records and her fears and her what-ifs. My stepfather was tying up loose ends in Las Vegas and would join her in a few days.

I would have many of these out-of-body, eat-a-rat-to-get-what-you-need, by-any-means-necessary experiences over the course of the next year. I would lie to my mother's friends about the state of her health. I'd squash rumors by configuring so many stories of varying shapes and sizes that I started listing them in Command Central to keep them straight. *Did I tell Frances this? Did I tell Grandpa that?*

I'd pretend to my own friends that I was dealing with it all like a black Martha Stewart, writing articles, making grapevine wreaths, dipping candles, baking bread, and making funky little pillows in my spare time. I made it seem perfectly normal to Christopher and Nicole that Granny lived with us when she was not feeling well and went back to her apartment to spend time with Papa John when she felt better.

I lied to Darnay that this wasn't too much to handle, determined to show him that I could seamlessly manage the sickness, the support, the kids, the meals, the freelance work, and the house and still be there for him. "It will be just the same as always."

But I told the biggest lie to myself. I said I could make all this go away. Eating the first rat and telling the first lie was the hardest. The next hundred lies started to go down like Reese's peanut butter cups. Soon I didn't feel it. I didn't feel much of anything. I just did it, one critter, one lie, one step at a time, until they all blurred together. Lies became the truth that kept me glued together.

THREE

Three days after she arrived back in Lansing, my mother and I sat in an oncologist's waiting room at the Michigan State University Clinical Center, armed with X rays, ultrasounds, and medical reports from the hospital in Las Vegas.

One of my friends who had been through a bout of breast cancer earlier that year and had referred us to the doctor warned me about the waiting room. "Some of the patients look like they escaped from a Polish death camp." The ten other people there were really sick. Some had lost their hair, one had a bandage taped tightly over his eye like a tic-tac-toe mark. A couple of patients were firmly attached to oxygen tanks.

The woman sitting directly in front of me had a duck-down buzz cut so faint that her hair seemed to have no color at all; her eyebrows had been drawn on by a really shaky hand, using what looked like a fat-tipped black marker. Her little white arms, which were exposed by her sleeveless shirt, showed inky, bruised veins. She caught me staring. "It was bad," she said, "but I have a port now. One stick and they're in."

17

I didn't know what a port was, but I jotted a note to myself in Command Central to ask the oncologist about it. If it made things better, then it might come in handy later.

When you sit in an oncologist's office with nothing else to do but read magazines with articles like "Living with Malignancy Today," there is the irresistible temptation to play the cancer guessing game. I found myself looking at the women's chests, trying to figure out if they had had a mastectomy or a lumpectomy, chemo or radiation, or both. I assumed that the man with the nasty, hacking cough and the dark green teeth had lung cancer. I nodded and smiled politely as I sized them up, and they nodded and smiled back as they tried to figure out who had cancer, my mother or me, and what kind. The man with the green teeth looked at my chest, zeroed in on my left breast, and I promptly crossed my arms over myself.

While they waited to be called in, they warmed up to each other, bonding by trading, like baseball cards, horror stories. "I've got a lung the size of a dime," the man with the mossy teeth said, and hacked up what I was sure was a piece of it, balling it up into a single-ply tissue.

"Shit, that ain't nothing," another patient said. Forming a huge fist and holding it out he said, "My prostate was swollen up to the size of a tomato on Miracle-Gro." The female patients were all too quiet, which led me to believe that their illnesses, like my mother's, were the types that were not to be discussed in mixed company.

I was fascinated in the same way that people are at the scene of a gruesome accident, wanting to look away but needing to see. But Mother refused to make eye contact with anyone in the room. She wanted nothing to do with it.

She picked up a few of the women's magazines, flipped through them, and put them down. She whistled. She talked about the office's wallpaper, which was covered with big pink, blue, and green cabbage-size flowers. The more I looked at them, the more they looked like swirls in motion. If chemotherapy caused nausea, I wondered if the other patients would look at the swirls and start projectile vomiting at any moment.

"Nicole needs some plaid pleated skirts for when school starts," my mother whispered. "Maybe we can stop by the store and pick some out when we leave here." It didn't seem to matter to her that it was the first week of August and the temperature outside was about ninety-nine degrees. It also didn't matter that little girls haven't worn plaid pleated skirts to school since 1965, unless they went to Our Lady of Perpetual Motion Immaculate Lamb of God the Nuns Will Smack You with a Ruler If You Pop Gum Catholic School.

Then she noticed the television and video monitor, and decided, "We should pick up some movies on the way home."

A nondescript nurse who smelled like vanilla extract and rubbing alcohol came out and introduced herself. She took the big medical envelope from me and showed us into the patient-education library. It was a sunny little room, with tables and pads of paper, pens, and plastic models of all manner of body parts, and she explained that we could "enjoy books and tapes, or check them out and keep them until your next visit."

The nurse suggested that my mother might really like the Bernie Segal tapes and videos, which describe visualization during chemo. "Patients love him," she said. It sounded a bit like Lamaze breathing to me—something to keep your mind busy while your ass is getting eaten alive. But I picked up the video and showed it to her.

"Look, we don't even have to go to the video store now," I whispered, louder than I meant to. Mother nudged me and accused me of having no manners.

The nurse laughed. She took us past more patients. It turned out that the sickest ones weren't in the waiting room but were hidden away in the back, like broken toys. The nurse led Mother to examining room number 3 to put her things down, then took her out to the scale. I suggested that she keep her shoes on and hold her purse to add a little weight. The nurse said, "107," and brought her back in.

"It looks like you are down ten pounds from when you were in the hospital, Earline," the nurse said as she reviewed the Las Vegas chart.

I made a note in my book in a section that I would later label "Weight." If she kept losing weight at the rate of ten pounds every two weeks, according to my calculations she'd be down to sixty pounds by her sixtieth birthday, on October 13.

Dr. Leahy came in a few minutes later. She was younger than I'd expected, in her mid-thirties, I guessed, making her just a year or so older than me. She had a shiny, light brown, Dutch-boy haircut, like Moe from the Three Stooges, that swung around when she moved.

The two of them made the required small talk. Mother introduced me as Baby.

"Ma, please," I whined.

I didn't mind being called Baby at home, in private, but as a thirty-five-year-old woman with a family of her own who was still trying to wrest away some independence, being called Baby in public, as if I was somebody's blue ribbon–winning pig at the county fair made me a little defensive. Cancer softened a lot of things between my mother and me, but being introduced as Baby wasn't one of them. I reintroduced myself loud and clear: "Andrea King Collier."

We shook hands. Mother told Dr. Leahy all about her grand-kids. The doctor was using the moment as an icebreaker, and Mother took the opportunity to avoid talking about her illness, as if she figured that if she didn't talk about it, maybe it wouldn't come up. She became very animated.

Over the years, I had seen her try to charm and entertain the friends and boyfriends of mine that she liked (woe to the ones that she didn't like). I saw right through what was going on. She was trying to convince Dr. Leahy that she was fine, and that the diagnosis had been a mistake. Someone so perky and alert couldn't possibly be as sick as the other people here.

Eventually Dr. Leahy got to the bottom line. She leaned in and took Mother's hand. "You know that you have cancer," she said, as if she were unfolding the most intimate of secrets to Mother.

"Yes," Mother reluctantly agreed, raising and lowering her tiny shoulders, sighing much like she had the night she'd called me. It was the sigh of a person who was resigning herself to some awful punishment. Mother looked at the doctor directly for a few seconds, then lowered her eyes and looked away, as if she was embarrassed that she was ill.

"What kind is it?" I asked, interrupting this moment that they seemed to be having.

"We really aren't sure about the site of origination yet," Dr. Leahy said, flipping through the charts.

"Based on what you have now, what kind do you think it is?" I would have settled for any reasonable guess so that my imagination could stop reeling at the possibilities.

My mother got quiet. She didn't care what kind it was. She never asked. It was just enough for her to know that it was cancer. Case closed. Like many women of her generation, cancer was always seen as an absolute death sentence and it was almost never discussed. When I was a kid, I remember that the adults would speak about it in hushed tones, if they talked about it at all. The person in question was long dead before anybody said the "C" word. I'm not sure that Mother had ever even known anybody who'd had cancer and had survived.

A few years before, she'd cared for my grandfather's only sibling, my uncle Harrison, when he was dying of cancer. She eventually found him residential hospice care, managed his affairs, and visited him every day until the end. Yet she never said that he had cancer. She'd only say, "He's sick. Really sick."

Most of us in the family knew, but we never said the words either. My grandfather, who played at being fragile better than anybody I've ever known, always maintained an as-need-to-know basis when it came to bad news. Because nobody was saying exactly what was wrong, Grandpa decided that Harrison, whom we all called Brother, must have had AIDS, because he was gay, which was something else we never talked about back then. We simply said Brother was "flamboyant."

When Grandpa asked Mother if Brother indeed had AIDS, she said no. This created more mystery and speculation than if she had just come clean and said he had pancreatic cancer. Now, as I sat with her and her doctor, I recognized that her handling of her uncle's cancer was a dress rehearsal for how she would deal with her own.

Early on she swore Darnay and me to secrecy. She didn't want anybody other than the two of us and John to know. She made us promise we wouldn't say anything to other family members until we knew what kind it was and how bad it was, then she became obsessed with not wanting anybody to know at all—never, if possible. "Even though they mean well, people say stupid things when they know you're sick," she'd said.

She may not have cared what kind of cancer it was, but it was all I could think about. I needed to know the name of the enemy in order to gird myself to help her fight it. I had kept myself sane while I waited for this first meeting with Dr. Leahy by reading anything on women's cancers that I could get my hands on. I went to the library and the American Cancer Society. I had my little notebook in hand, ready to look up the statistics and survival rates, based on what Dr. Leahy told us.

"It's gynecological in origin, clearly. Maybe cervical. Maybe uterine," she said. She measured her words like fine ingredients, doling them out in tiny increments. Based on what I'd read over the last few days, if it absolutely had to be cancer, I was praying for cervical or uterine, hoping that somehow we were catching it early. Early detection of these two cancers meant a better chance of survival than ovarian cancer, which had the most dismal survival rates. I was relieved, finding satisfaction in the fact that she had talked about cervical and uterine cancer. I relaxed for the first time since getting the call: *The doctors here say they think I have some kind of cancer.* Then Dr. Leahy said, "Possibly ovarian." That hit me like a ton of bricks.

Ovarian cancer is called the silent killer because it offers symptoms that could be attributed to hundreds of other illnesses and maladies. Little can be offered in the way of early detection. By the time it is found, it is usually pretty advanced, and very few clinical trials have shown any real promise.

"That's the worst," I said, forgetting that my mother was in the room hiding from any information that would help her understand what was happening to her. She cut me a look that I had seen many times before. I was becoming one of those people she was avoiding. I was one of the people who say stupid things around people who are sick.

"Let's not jump ahead of ourselves," Dr. Leahy said. Her voice was like soft music. Whatever she said sounded a little less frightful because she composed her sentences with just the right amount of compassion.

"We'll get you in with the surgeon, and see what we have. Then we'll make a determination of how advanced it is so we can plan a course of treatment," she said, trying to calm my mother, who had shut down. She was whistling, looking around the room, swinging her legs. It took me a minute to figure out what she was singing. Then it came to me: "I whistle a happy tune, so no one will suspect I'm afraid."

23

Her retreat made me more fearless on her behalf. My questions became more aggressive, my note taking more furious. I am sure that family members like me are a nightmare to an oncologist. Having just enough information to be dangerous and annoying, I declared myself an essential member of Mother's medical team, spewing out the names of all the chemotherapy drugs I had ever heard of. "What about cocktails? What about Cisplatin? What about trials? When can we start?"

"As I said, first we need to know what we are dealing with and what stage it is," Dr. Leahy said, addressing my mother, the real patient, who I was convinced was mentally at the farmers' market by now because she was not participating in the discussion. She had received too much information and couldn't take in any more. Occasionally she'd repeat a word or two to prove to us that she was keeping track of the conversation. But she wasn't.

I assured the doctor that it couldn't possibly be advanced cancer because annual Paps would have caught anything abnormal. "Right?" I was looking to her for assurance and she was looking at my mother, who had all but disappeared, as she sat on the edge of the examining table.

"Well, Paps normally do pick up cervical and uterine changes. Have you been getting your annual Paps, Earline?" Dr. Leahy asked.

"Of course, she has," I blurted out. Mother never answered, too busy whistling her happy tune.

The doctor walked over to Mother and put an arm around her. "Earline, when was the last time you had a Pap, or a mammogram?" she asked, soft and patient. There was no judgment in her voice.

"A little while ago," Mother mumbled, staring at her swinging legs. She'd been caught with her hand in the cookie jar.

My heart was beating faster now. I felt hot. All along, I had been counting on this, hanging on to it like a lifeline from the moment she had told me she had cancer. It couldn't be too bad because we were catching it early. There was so much they could do with cancer if it was caught early. All my books said so.

"I had a mammogram and an . . . exam when I retired," Mother said softly, now looking helplessly at me. *Don't be mad, please.*

She retired from the telephone company just before I got married, after thirty-five years. "You retired nine years ago. That can't be right." I must have been shouting, because I could feel Dr. Leahy watching us.

Mother looked at the doctor. "I guess it was nine years ago." She shrugged.

She hadn't had a Pap or a mammogram in nearly a decade, but she said she'd had a series of upper and lower gastrointestinal tests and a colorectal exam a year ago when she had been feeling some abdominal pressure and bloating just before she moved to Vegas. She had been given a clean bill of health—no cancer or anything like that. The internist had thought she might have the beginning of an ulcer, so he had prescribed Tagamet and told her to drink milk every day, she said. But she'd had none of the tests that would have picked up this cancer early.

Dr. Leahy had Mother lie down on the table and pull up her top. I was surprised to see that her belly was swollen. The doctor tapped it with her index finger and took a few notes. "Does the swelling make you uncomfortable, Earline?"

Mother shrugged again.

Over my years as a freelance writer I'd done tons of health stories on early detection. I've spoken to groups, raging and beating my chest, about issues of access for the poor and underserved, but it had never occurred to me that there was more to good health care than access. Or that my own mother, who had great insurance, enough money to afford the extras of care, access to doctors and medical centers, and was armed with a daughter who was a walking encyclopedia of medical information on any diagnostic test you could name, would not have had a regular Pap or a mammogram. I didn't understand why she wouldn't have gotten herself checked out.

"I was afraid that they might find something," she said.

I was shaking with rage. I had needed this to be somebody or something's fault. My stepfather. Me. The stress of the move to Las Vegas. Being separated from us. I had been ready to sue someone who might have misdiagnosed her. But now, with all the cards on the table, I realized who the real villain was. If she died, if I lost her, it was . . . her fault.

Cancer, at least in its early stages, is a raw, angry disease. Everybody shakes their fist at the sky and asks why: "Why me?" "Why her?" "Why now?" Lots of time is spent being angry with the disease for eating away at you, and angry with people for not knowing what to say, and not knowing if you should be pissed off at God for giving you this to deal with. I'd read that those feelings were normal in the early days. I could expect that. But now I was angry with the patient for letting this thing sneak up and grab her. It was not my finest moment. I stayed angry on and off for a long time.

FOUR

Thanks to a cancellation, Mother's surgery was moved up to eleven A.M. the next day. It happened so fast that there was no time to fret over the possibilities. That night she insisted that we go over everything that she had in a big golden envelope with my name written on it.

"Do we have to do this now?" I pleaded. "Can't we do it when you come home?" It seemed to be begging bad luck. We needed good luck.

"I want to do it now. Just to be sure," she said to me.

We went over all her papers while we sat on the bed. Stocks, bonds, wills, insurance. She had insisted that all new accounts be set up jointly with me so that I could pay the bills and act on her behalf.

The next morning we ate breakfast with the children, took them to day care, then went to the hospital. We laughed and made silly jokes. We cracked up at the thin cotton gown she had to wear, and the shot in the butt she got to help her relax. I held her hand.

Just before they wheeled her into surgery, she asked the nurse, "You think they can do a little tummy tuck while they're in there?" And off they went.

John's bus from Las Vegas came in just an hour before the surgery, so he took a cab to the hospital. He was grayer than I remembered. I gave him a quick rundown of what had happened so far. "They think the surgery will take a couple of hours," I said.

He decided that since he was in the hospital killing time, he would mosey on down to the emergency room to see about a nagging pain he had in his neck. "A car hit mine from behind before I left." Then he was gone.

People came and went in waves in the surgery waiting room. As in the oncologist's waiting room, people started to bond. They shared their stories. They cried. They talked as optimistically as possible. There were heart surgeries, kids getting tubes put in their ears, biopsies, hip replacements.

I brought work to keep my mind off waiting: correspondence, magazines that I needed to catch up on, a book on the latest cancer treatments. But I couldn't concentrate. I watched the people instead. For every person who sat in the waiting room, there was someone under general anesthesia. All surgery is major surgery and every operation includes a risk that the person might not make it. People go into the dentist's office and die, so anything is possible. All of us knew it, and a nervous buzz filled the room as we all tried to look normal and confident that everything was going to be okay.

A senior volunteer sat at a desk, and when she got a call from the operating room, she'd call out a patient's name. The family members would go up to the desk and get the news, then go off to the recovery room. For the most part, things were going well for everyone. But a few times, the volunteer called out a name and a different person whisked the family members away. Once, after this happened, I heard piercing, soul-beating wails come from down the hall. "Lord Jesus," one woman cried out. "No, Lord Jesus, please."

After that, we waiting-room slaves weren't quite so sure that we wanted our husband, mother, sister, or child's name called. We jumped every time the phone rang. Time passed so slowly. Volunteers came and went.

Three hours later, with Mother still in the operating room, John finally reappeared with a huge neck brace. "I have whiplash," he announced.

He started telling me the details, but I wasn't interested. "Not now," I said.

Finally, the volunteer called out, "Earline Terry."

We got up and met a nurse who led us to a consultation room. It had tables and comfortable blue cloth-covered chairs. The room was darker than I expected, with dim, recessed lighting. You could lose all sense of day and night in a room like this. I felt a knowing chill. We, too, had been whisked away.

I'd been here before. On a scorching-hot August day eight years before, I had waited in a room like this with my grandfather, my mother, and her sister after taking my grandmother to the hospital in an ambulance. She had suddenly taken ill the day after being involved in a minor fender bender.

I'd gone over to visit my grandparents that afternoon. When I got there, Grandma was in bed. Even at seventy-one she never got in bed in the middle of the day. She never put quilts over herself in the stifling heat of August. She never asked my grandfather to make her soup and serve it to her in his favorite bowl. I got the feeling that she might be slipping away in front of me and that things were going too wrong too fast.

I was so scared. One minute we were laughing and telling funny little stories, the next minute everything flipped upside down. As I sat on the side of Grandma's bed, talking to Mother on the phone, poised to tell her that we needed a doctor fast,

Grandma grabbed my hand. Every time I tried to ask for help, she would squeeze it gently. "Hang up now," she whispered. And I did.

Within a half hour, my grandfather, aunt, and mother were sitting in the emergency room at the hospital. I had to explain why I hadn't told her while I had her on the phone.

We waited for an agonizing hour that felt like four. They all held hands and prayed together, but I didn't. I quietly slipped out into the hallway.

I had already said the prayers that they were now saying. Before the ambulance arrived, I had knelt out in the grass rocking myself and saying, "Hail Mary Full of Grace Angel of God Our Father Who Art Jesus Loves the Little Children," a nonstop chant of every prayer I could think of that might save her. *Faster, faster, pray faster.*

I felt the presence of someone, one of the neighbors, I thought, kneeling down next to me and holding me while I rocked. She said, "Don't pray that you can change what's happening now. Pray that you can be strong enough to accept what will happen next."

When I looked up, nobody was there, but the struggle that I had felt and the frantic need to pray faster was gone. I knew in that moment that it was over. I left the consultation room because I didn't want them to see in my eyes what I knew. Grandma couldn't be saved because she was already gone.

My mother followed me out into the hall and shook me by my shoulders. "She's going to be okay, isn't she?" she asked.

"No," I said. "She's gone." It didn't come out right. I had never wanted to be the one to say it, especially not to my mother. Let the doctor break the news, I thought.

"She's not gone. You're wrong," she said. "Don't say it again. Never." Her eyes were wild and angry and full of tears. "She can't be gone." We looked at each other for a long time before either of us spoke.

"Why didn't you tell me that she was so sick?" she asked, desperate.

"Ma, I tried. She wanted to leave on her own terms," I said, sounding wiser than I normally did at twenty-seven. I was known in my family as the smart one, sometimes the smart-assed one, but not the wise one. What I said was so deep that it even scared me.

Mother shook her head, shaking off my words, and went back inside the consultation room. I didn't go back in until the emergency-room doctor arrived.

"I'm sorry. Really sorry," he said. "We just couldn't bring her back."

I could hardly hear him over the cries of my family.

"The paramedics did all they could, but couldn't resuscitate her. She was probably gone before she got here."

When he said that, my mother looked up at me as if I had stolen something irreplaceable from her. I got my purse, walked out, and kept on walking.

Now, years later, I was in a room just like it, praying that there would be no sad, bad news.

The surgeon came in dressed in a fresh set of blue scrubs. He was what my grandmother would have called a tall, cool drink of water. He had to be older than he looked, sort of fresh-faced and freckled, with longish red hair. He had an Opie Taylor thing working. He probably grew the mustache to be taken seriously. He shook hands with us and started right in. No warm-up act here.

"She has stage four ovarian cancer," he said.

I held my breath. John had no idea what that meant. I looked at him and said, "This is bad." But John didn't believe me. What could I know?

"Doctor?" he asked, wringing his hands, twisting his wedding band.

"It isn't what we'd hoped for," the surgeon said.

"What did you have to take out?" I asked.

"It would be easier, quite frankly, to tell you what we left in. The surgery was very extensive."

He talked with his hands. They were long and thin, like those of an artist or a concert pianist, almost delicate. As he explained how the cancer had spread throughout Mother's reproductive organs, choking them off before spreading to something else vital, his hands opened and shut. He seemed fascinated by his own gestures. I found myself watching his hands much more than his eyes as he talked.

"We had to do a radical hysterectomy," he said.

Hysterectomies are so common that it seems to be the remedy for almost all female ailments, for fibroids, for cysts for . . . cancer. I was expecting that, even though Mother and I hadn't talked about it. I wondered how she would react to losing so much of herself without giving permission. Go to sleep with your ovaries and fallopian tubes, your uterus, all the things that biology said made you a woman. Wake up with all your plumbing gone.

He used the back of his hand to show us how he had also had to remove parts of the inner lining of the abdomen, which he said was "full of cancer cells" that would have spread. "We also had to drain quite a bit of fluid. Ovarian cancer produces a fair amount of buildup. So this should give her some relief."

I nodded, still looking at the back of his hand. There was some good news in this story, thank God. "So you got everything?"

He was silent for a minute, looking up for the first time since he'd outlined on his hand the surgery. "No," he said. "We still couldn't get all of the tumor. She simply couldn't take any more. We had to stop."

So what was the point? "How does that work? It just stays in there and kills her?" I was leaning into him. At that moment, John must have gotten it. I heard him start to whimper, next to me. I didn't look up because I was stuck on the movements of the surgeon's hands. All the truths seemed to lie in the creases and folds of his palms, in his knuckles, in his fingers.

He held them out again, palms up. "There is still some tumor, about the size of a walnut," he said, circling the center of one palm with the fingers of the other hand.

"Once the surgeon does what he can do, the oncologist will sometimes recommend chemotherapy to reduce the size of the tumor. If that works, then the surgeon can go in and try to take it out."

"More surgery?"

"Yes," he said. "There is something else." His hands stopped moving, and my eyes met his. "There was so much damage to her colon and her intestines that we did a colostomy," he said. "When we do a colostomy, we reroute the intestine to a hole that we make in the patient's side, called a stoma." Then he made a little circle about the size of a quarter with his fingers and moved the circle to the side of his abdomen.

"Colostomy," I repeated.

"There was enough left to reconnect at some point, if she were to go into remission. That would require surgery. We might need to go in and drain her of fluid periodically, if her abdomen builds up again. She'll also need another surgery after treatment to see if it was really successful. So there could be a few more surgeries," he said, counting out the possible operations on the tips of his fingers.

This was the first really hopeful thing that he said, the first glimmer that she might be okay. "That's good news, right?"

"The good news is that she made it through surgery," he said. "Now she has to make it through the night."

It was bad enough that my worst fears had been confirmed, that it was ovarian cancer—advanced ovarian cancer. I was slightly prepared for that, at least. Leahy had told us that it was definitely one of the possibilities. But it had never occurred to me that she might not make it through the surgery.

"There is the possibility that such a comprehensive surgery could kill her. That's the first concern with an operation like this. It was very extensive."

John fell apart. He started to cry loudly and walked out of the room with his neck brace firmly in place.

"Should I continue?" the surgeon asked, seeing that I was making no moves to go after John.

For all of Dr. Leahy's soft, soothing explanations and hand holding, the surgeon was one who, excuse the pun, cut to the chase. He was a skilled technician who did his job and came in to give you the details. And I had no intention of missing anything just because John couldn't take any more.

"So what does all this mean?" I asked. "In terms of getting better and starting treatment?"

He had defined his boundaries as a surgeon long ago, refusing to speculate on any other aspect of the treatment. I think he would have talked all night long about dissection and vivisections, -ostomies and -ectomies. But the moment I asked questions beyond what parts he took out and why he took them out, he shut down.

"I'm just the surgeon," he said as he turned to go. "I will be following up with your mother on how she does postop. The things you want to know about prognosis and treatment are out of my area. These are questions for Dr. Leahy."

I stood. He patted my shoulder, which is probably a grand gesture of compassion for a surgeon. "It's a lot to absorb, I know."

"When can we go in and see her?"

He said that the nurse would come get us as soon as she came out of recovery. "She'll be in intensive care until we get her stabilized." Then he walked away.

FIVE

After I called Darnay to check in, I found John outside, leaning against the building in the clear summer night, having a smoke. "I didn't know she was that sick, Ann. I swear, I didn't know," he said.

"I didn't either." It was the first time we had looked each other in the eye since we'd had our rough-and-tumble battle when I was twelve. Then I reached out and hugged him. It was awkward and strained, but it was the only gesture I knew to give. The whole time we had known each other, we had never touched; it was a part of our unspoken truce. It occurred to me at that moment that I could afford to be a little more generous. This would be hard on all of us and it would take all of us to get through it. "It will be okay," I reassured him. We stood outside in the night breeze in silence for a while.

An hour or so later, someone took us to the ICU, where we found her hooked up to machines and things that went beep in the night. I couldn't see the lines that connected her to the monitors because she was wrapped from head to toe in cream-colored blankets.

"She's lost so much blood," the intensive-care nurse said. "They get cold when they lose so much blood." Mother looked so tiny. How could she fight when she had all her parts taken out? Did they even leave her enough to put up a good fight?

Dr. Leahy came in, and I introduced her to John. She took us to the ICU waiting room to explain exactly what we could expect. My new life was going to be full of waiting rooms.

"I know you talked to the surgeon, and he told you about these critical hours after surgery," she said, looking from me to John, and back again. "If she comes out of that okay, she'll need aggressive chemotherapy as soon as possible."

I took notes on everything she said.

"If she makes it through the surgery, then she'll be fine after the chemotherapy, right?" I asked, holding my breath for the right answer.

"Truth?"

When anybody says "Truth?," you know the truth is not going to be what you'd hoped for. The truth is going to knock you out. The truth is going to be a hole that you fall into. And so it was.

"Unlike other cancers, ovarian cancer is a tough one. By the time it's diagnosed, it is very difficult to treat." The five-year survival rates were very low she said. "She may even decide that she doesn't want to do the chemo."

"So, if the chemo doesn't work, or if she decides not to have it?" I asked.

"Maybe a year. Once it gets going, ovarian cancer is very fast-moving."

It was easier for me to hear that she might not make it through the night. I couldn't understand not fighting. It was too hard to believe that with all the science and technology, all the chemo cocktails that were out there, that we would just be marking time.

"With all due respect," I said, "we plan to keep her here a lot longer than that, so get your best chemo ready."

The doctor took my hand, and smiled. "Agreed," she said.

She answered a few more questions, then went back into ICU. We followed behind her. She looked at her watch. It was eleven o'clock, she said, and suggested that we go home and get some rest. "Earline will be asleep for the rest of the night."

I couldn't think of leaving my mother. If she were to die that night, she wouldn't die with strangers. I parked myself in the big recliner next to her bed. I wanted to touch her, but was afraid that I'd wake her

"We're gonna get you well, Mommy, but you have to hang on. You gotta fight, okay?" I begged. I reminded her that Nicole and Chris wouldn't be able to stand it if I came home and had to tell them that she was gone. "And I'm not ready. You can't leave me."

I bargained and negotiated. "If you come back, I won't get mad when you call me Baby around other people." I promised her that I would wear all the suits she bought me. Then I thought I heard her groan.

"She's not in any pain, is she?" I asked the nurse who came in to heap more blankets on her.

"No way. These are some serious drugs your momma has in her. She's feeling nooooo pain, honey."

John was wiping his eyes with a tissue. "I'm going to drive back to Gary. You'll have my number if you need to reach me," he announced from out of nowhere.

"What?"

There he stood in his whiplash collar, planning what would be the first of many escapes. "This is too much. I need to be with my folks," he said, wiping sweat off his brow with his sleeve. It never occurred to him to have his folks come to him.

"I feel so useless," he said.

"I wonder why," I said, low, so he couldn't hear me. The nurse looked up from adjusting the IV line. The truce was broken. From that moment, whenever I looked at him, it would be through squinting eyes.

I wanted to scuff him up for even thinking about leaving now. I wanted to grab him by his whiplash collar and run him around in little circles for watching her get grayer and sicker and not making her go to a doctor sooner. I wanted to banish him for all that and for the things I'd hated him for when I was a kid, mainly marrying my mom and taking me away from a perfectly normal life. All my baggage came right up with all my fear.

I got up and moved quickly toward him. Just as I was leading him out into the hall to curse him out, I heard a tiny voice say, "John . . .

"Don't even think about it," she said, having heard it all.

I let go of him, and we both turned around. "And what's that thing around your neck?" she asked.

I left them alone. Her voice was muted under the blankets, so I couldn't hear everything, just bits and pieces. She was railing at him the best she could under the haze of pain meds.

"If you think . . . If you leave . . . get all of your stuff . . . you are pretty damn crazy. Pretty damn sad." I could swear I heard her use the "F" word.

I have felt the razor-tongued wrath of Earline Comer Terry over the years. You don't want to be in the room when it happens even if it's not happening to you. And with a mind like an elephant, she was going to stretch this out for a long time.

Just as I'd known that my grandmother was not going to make it back, I knew at that moment that she was going to make it through the night, if only to make his life a little special. All was right with the world—at least for the moment.

SIX

After the surgery, I became an obsessed collector of cancer information. My copy of comedienne Gilda Radner's book, *It's Always Something,* about her battle with ovarian cancer, went everywhere with me. I'd go to the library and search the databases, jotting down notes and preparing questions for our next visit with Dr. Leahy. When Command Central spilled over with notes and newspaper clips, magazine articles, and information on clinical trials, I added a Command Central II and carried both in my ever-present book bag. I went through three notebooks in the first month.

During those first few days after the surgery, I'd duck out of the hospital while Mother was sleeping and head to the American Cancer Society to look at tapes, copy more articles, and talk to people about programs and support groups like Y-Me and Looking Good Feeling Good. I had my work cut out for me if I was going to convince her to go to any of them, but I knew that I would be relentless in trying.

After staying out as long as I could without being missed, I'd go back to the hospital and watch her until visiting hours were over. I'd go home dog-tired, cook for the kids, and hear everybody's story of daily life. "Chris fell down at day care," Nicole said one time. Chris, with his bright, shiny eyes and long eyelashes, flashed me a baby smile and pointed to the big goose egg on his forehead. "Boom."

Darnay would talk about work, knowing that I wasn't really paying attention, and I would nod politely. Someone would whine about having to eat yucky vegetables, and we'd laugh. I was grateful to have someplace to go after the hospital, thankful for a world of finger painting, hair combing, bumps on heads, and crusty little noses, a world that wasn't steeped in the urgencies of life and death.

"When can we go to the hospital to see Granny?" Nicole had asked every day since the surgery. I had been worried about how all this would affect them. We didn't know how it would turn out, and, as Mother had said early on, it could end up very badly. How would I get them through this? It pressed on my mind so much that I asked a counselor I found through the American Cancer Society just how much I should tell them. Christopher was easier. He lived in his two-year-old world. But Nicole had been so close to Mother. What did she need to know?

"Tell her what she needs to know at the time," the counselor said. "Kids pick up on things. They'll ask what they want to know. So when she asks, tell the truth." That's what we did. She didn't have the big life-and-death questions at first. They were little questions. "Why is Papa John here?" "If Granny and Papa John have an apartment, why is she coming back here?"

It was odd; the one question I thought she would ask, she never did. I held my breath waiting for the day when Nicole would ask if Granny was going to get well, but it never occurred to her that Granny wouldn't get well.

We made sure that the kids talked to her on the phone every day. "Do they give you shots, Granny?" "Is the food good?" They sent artwork and handmade cards. She, in return, would send me on shopping sprees for stuffed animals and juice boxes, videos and coloring books.

Darnay was starting to feel the strain of doing double duty between work and keeping things together at home with the children. I was exhausted from being at the hospital all the time. When I finally got home, I'd fall asleep in the middle of conversations with him, sitting on the stairs. Just to get enough energy to crawl up to bed was like trying to beat my wings hard enough to fly. When I got in bed, I'd fall asleep right away knowing that I had to get up and start it all over the next day.

SEVEN

As part of an effort to have a life that wasn't totally swallowed up by sickness and in-laws, Darnay took up golf that summer. He had no way of knowing that chasing a little white ball around a manicured field for hours with old men wearing ugly plaid pants would keep him sane in the middle of such chaos.

The day after Mother's surgery he arranged for a baby-sitter and went golfing right after work. Out on the course, he felt a little straining and tightening in his abdomen. "Then I swear I heard a little snap," he told me when he got home. He lifted his golf shirt to show me a noticeable bulge in his otherwise toned stomach.

"Do you see it?" he asked.

I did see it and started to cry like a person whose puppy got run over.

"Damn, does it look that bad?" he asked, astonished to have drawn such a hysterical response from me.

When I looked at him, all I saw was cancer. This little bulge, about the size of a walnut, was some fast-moving growth that would sweep through his body and kill him dead by the day after tomorrow, leaving me a young widow with two unruly kids and no stable income.

Since my mother had gotten sick, everything I read, every show I watched, everybody I talked to was an omen of some lurking malignancy to come. The cancer abyss was swallowing me whole. Not only was I starting to hear the first ticking of the time bomb of cancer that I was sure rested in me, but I saw it in everyone else. Simply enjoying a day in the sun represented melanomas to me. Darnay's tiny bump was just another thing pulling me under.

I was so lost in my own fears that I did the only thing I could think to do. I cried, which was pretty damn unnerving for a guy who had simply lifted his golf shirt to show me his belly.

Two days later, Darnay and I were in yet another doctor's office, a hernia specialist referred to us by our HMO doctor. Yes, there is such a thing as a hernia doctor. The HMO doctor had told us that the bulge looked like an umbilical hernia, but since he was not a specialist, he was shipping us off to the Hernia King, who could both diagnose and operate, if necessary.

The Hernia King came in, introduced himself and shook my hand, then Darnay's. He didn't have the slender hands that I now associated with surgeons. He had the giant hands and hairy knuckles of a television wrestler. His fingers were so squat and muscular that they almost seemed to have biceps and triceps of their own.

What the Hernia King lacked in sheer finger beauty he made up for in personality. He and Darnay talked like guys having a brewski in a sports bar. "Hey, fella, what you got going on there?" he asked, slapping Darnay on his back.

"When did you first notice this?" he asked as he felt up Darnay's belly, circling the little bulge.

"On the golf course," Darnay said.

From there they spoke in a foreign language that I didn't understand. As they volleyed back and forth, I realized that I was witnessing a testosterone meeting.

"What do you shoot?" Hernia King said, raising Darnay's arm and lowering it, making the bulge dance.

"About a seven," Darnay said as he watched his belly.

"My game has been in the crapper this year. Then I got some Pings," the Hernia King said. "I just got some Callaways," Darnay said proudly, in the way that men talk about the big fish they've caught.

Then off they went talking about some woman named Bertha. I gathered that there was a whole family of women named Bertha and each was bigger and better than the last. There was someone named Big Bertha and some new woman named Big-Ass Bertha. Later I would learn that Big-Ass Bertha was a golf club with a head the size of a mutant watermelon, which made it impossible for you to miss the little white ball.

"Give us a cough," the Hernia King said.

Darnay coughed.

"Good. Again," he said. "You ever go to the courses up north?"

"Not yet, but I am planning on it." Darnay coughed again.

The Hernia King had him lie down on the examining table, and he rubbed his hand across Darnay's stomach, searching and feeling. He started thumping like Dr. Leahy had done during that first exam with my mother. I knew that move, it was the cancer move. I felt tears roll down my face again.

"Sit up now," the Hernia King said. He helped Darnay up and held his left shoulder in a firm grip with his left hand. Then, in a quick gesture that gave no forewarning, he poked two fingers on his right hand into Darnay's belly, the way I do when I make bread from scratch and want to make sure that the dough has doubled.

45

In what looked like carefully choreographed Fred and Ginger dance steps, Darnay, in reflex, took a swing at the Hernia King. "What the . . ."

Without missing a step, the Hernia King let go of Darnay's shoulder and caught the punch in the palm of his big wrestler's hand. He was smiling. "That was good."

"What the hell was good about that?" Darnay was not smiling. I knew the look on his face. He was trying to decide whether he should take another swing at him. "That hurt."

"Umbilical hernia," the Hernia King said and patted Darnay's shoulder. "We have to go in and patch it up."

"What does that do for golf?" Darnay asked. Threatened with losing valuable time on the links, my husband had forgotten all about wanting to kick the Hernia King's ass.

"You'll be off the course for about six to eight weeks. Work too," the King of All That Is Hernia said as he made notes in the metal chart.

⤳

There was no time to regroup; within two days we were at the hospital for his surgery. I had decided that we wouldn't tell my mother. Where I had been too naive to be truly afraid on the day of her surgery, this time I was keenly aware of all that could go wrong.

I cried from the moment they handed me his watch, his wallet, and his wedding band to the time that the volunteer called out his name postsurgery. I moved to the desk awaiting the news of his freak accidental death.

"He's fine," a nurse said and took me back to recovery, where he was in bed looking dazed but happily sipping a ginger ale.

"They won't let me go home until they know I can pee," he slurred with a big dopey grin on his face.

I pulled the nurse aside and asked, "Why does he sound like that?"

"He is," she said, "high as a kite." As much as I have come to associate hospitals and surgery with near-death experiences, I also now associate them with serious drugs that make you forget that they have just cut your stomach open. Where were these drugs when I had my kids?

"I need more pop, Ann. I have to make a pee or they won't let me go," he whined.

"That's right, sweetie, no pee and you're here with me all night," the nurse said.

"Give me some more pop, now." The pressure of an old woman he didn't know standing over him waiting for him to make water in something that looked like a Tupperware pitcher made his kidneys shut down. He drank water. He drank more pop. He ate Popsicles. No pee.

I tried to negotiate his release by promising that I would make sure that he peed when he got home. They weren't having it. In fact, the nurse looked at her watch and said, "If you don't do it in a few minutes, I'm going to send you up to a regular room. I'm going to need this bed."

And so he was admitted to a room right next to my mother's. The jig was up.

I went to Mother's room to break the news while they settled him in. She was in particularly good spirits. "I thought I wouldn't see you until tonight. Why are you back so soon?"

"Darnay had surgery today. I didn't want to worry you."

"Is he . . . ?" Her eyes filled with tears, just as mine had. Everything was bad news.

"He's fine," I was pleased to report. "But they won't let him go home until he pees. And he is not good at following orders. He's in the room next door."

I moved back and forth attending to each one's needs and passing messages on little notepads that the nurses gave me. Darnay and Mother started shouting out to each other and calling each other on the phone. I was embarrassed, but I was glad that they were alive and feeling well enough to be ridiculous. Good moments had become premium for us all.

"Hey, what you doing in there?" Darnay said.

"Waiting on a pizza and a beer," Mother answered.

"Send some over when it comes, okay?"

The hospital staff and the other patients were not amused. They finally gave up and released Darnay without the pee, but with full instructions on what to do if he didn't in the next few hours. Something was said about bringing him back and shoving a catheter up him.

As I drove about three miles per hour to avoid bumps and potholes, I explained where they wanted to put the catheter. His urge finally kicked in.

"Can you wait until we get home?" I asked.

"No. I have to go. Bad."

I pulled over behind a building, and got him out, holding him up to make sure that he didn't fall down or pass out. And at long last, he went and went and went. What a pitiful situation. All I could do was laugh. And laugh. I hadn't had anything to laugh about in a while and knew that I probably wouldn't for a long time.

He fell asleep as soon as I got him back in the car, snoring and holding his stomach. I just laughed some more.

EIGHT

A week later, I brought Mother home. I was so grateful to have them both safely home, under our roof again, but it didn't take long to figure out that my patients were more than a handful. There I was with a two-year-old son who was 85 percent potty trained on Tuesdays and Thursdays, a six-year-old daughter who was using my distraction as an excuse to pull off all manner of capers, and two of the walking wounded—neither of whom knew the first thing about being well behaved.

The little people were easy to manage, relatively speaking, because they went to day care, and wanted nothing but peanut butter sandwiches and Happy Meals. The adults were another story.

After a few days of being immobilized, my mother sent me out with a long list—pain prescriptions, Pepsi, chocolate candies, potato chips—so that she and Darnay, who also had marching orders to stay put, could escape from the house unnoticed. There is something about being told that you can't go anywhere that makes you want to run for it.

As soon as they were sure I was gone, they somehow got dressed, maneuvered down the stairs, and got into our stick-shift Chevy. Darnay was at the wheel of the getaway vehicle and Ma Barker helped guide him by looking out of the side-view mirror as he backed down the driveway. They were both too sore from their abdominal surgeries to turn around and look out of the back window.

They claimed that they were "doing just fine, thank you very much" until they hit the hard dip at the end of the drive-way, which shook all their stuffing loose. When I got home, they were still sitting in the car, parked half on the street and half in the drive, howling and moaning. Their powerful pain killers were a full driveway, four steps, and a locked house away.

"What took you so long? We could have died out here," Mother said.

NINE

Although he was constantly cranky after the surgery, Darnay knew that his immobility would pass and he took the setback in stride. But Mother took an emotional turn for the worse that day. She grew quiet and withdrawn, not even making attempts to hide the fact that she wasn't eating. She took to her bed, and seldom ventured downstairs to watch television or to play with the kids. Most of the time she pretended that she was asleep, but I could hear her crying behind her closed door. It tore me apart.

I alternated between trying to give her the space she needed to grieve for all she had lost and bursting in like a high school cheerleader with pom-poms in hand. I'd spew the facts and figures about cancer survival I had learned and that were keeping me going, handing her books from the stack I had by the bed. She'd hand them back to me, or I'd find them in the middle of the floor. I guessed that she was throwing them out of the bed when I left.

Every day I would come in with some new article, and she would turn them away. "Maybe tomorrow, okay?" she'd say.

I didn't give up. I continued to push her to read. "It really will help you to understand the things that the doctor says."

She'd look at me as if I was from some far-off planet. "I'm tired now. Can we do this tomorrow?"

I must admit that I was still simmering a bit because she hadn't taken care of herself. Every day, in my mind, I heard Dr. Leahy asking her about her regular checkups, but I hadn't said anything about it to her.

"You know, Ma, people don't die because they know what's happening. They die because they don't know. They die because they don't believe. You have to believe. You have to want to know." I had been wanting to say this to her for some time, but when it came out, it made me feel like I was worth about ten cents. I immediately wanted to take it back. Not because I didn't mean it, because I did. But because it sounded nasty and judgmental.

Who was I? I was just the girl on the sidelines, turning flips. I was the backseat driver. She was the one who was looking her mortality in the eye. No matter what "could have, should have" mumbo jumbo was bouncing around in my head, I didn't have to live with cancer. She did.

I left her to her thoughts, too embarrassed even to apologize.

"Granny cries a lot," Christopher said. "Did we do something bad?"

I explained that being so tired made Granny a little upset, but it was nothing that anybody had done. "Everything is going to be just fine. You'll see," I said. Christopher seemed to accept that better than I did.

やや

A few days later, a strange, pixie-haired woman with chubby cheeks and china-blue saucer eyes appeared at our house. All big teeth and round vowels, she introduced herself to Mother. "Hi, I'm Ginger, your home health nurse. Dr. Leahy's office assigned me."

She might as well have said, "Hi, Earline, I am the grim reaper, and I've come forth to carry you home."

Mother clicked her teeth like castanets and let out a faint hiss.

"How are you, Earline? I can call you Earline?" Ginger asked, taking a seat on the edge of Mother's bed.

"Surely," Mother said, squinting at her.

"Surely," was Earline-talk for go to hell, kiss my stretch-marked butt, eat chitterlings, and die. "Surely" was code for "Call me whatever you like, but, Miss Home Health Nurse, you don't ever have to call me again."

When I was little, I talked in code like that, but my word was "delicious." If I hated what you cooked, I would say, "Ooooh, that's so delicious." Okra was delicious. Lima beans were really delicious. For me, "delicious" meant that you couldn't force-feed it to me on an ice cream cone.

I watched as Miss Ginger attempted small talk with my mother. Mama, in turn, shut her out like a Hall of Fame pitcher.

"I'll come by and take your blood pressure, check your vitals, and make sure that you have enough pain pills to keep you comfortable," Ginger said. She wove in bits and pieces of her own life story while talking about my mother's care, treatment, and recovery. Ginger said that she had struggled with anorexia and bulimia, but was in a heavy-duty eating phase now. She had two kids, a first husband who had died of a heart attack, and a second one who'd died of non-Hodgkin's lymphoma. She was dating her second husband's doctor now.

"You'll be having chemo soon. Take your medications way before the pain sets in. It becomes very hard to control once it kicks in. Love your pajamas. Let me show you how to take care of your stoma," she said, referring to the colostomy site. Everything sounded like one long, running-together sentence.

My mother's eyelids fluttered. "I'm sleepy. I probably need to rest now," she said, one eyebrow raised. Then she flopped back on the bed and pretended to fall instantly asleep. She was snoring. Loudly. That's all she wrote. Mother had used up all the graciousness and politeness that she felt could be expected from a stage four cancer patient. So I whisked Ginger and her medical bag down the stairs and out to the door.

"Well, that went well, don't you think?" Ginger asked. Her eyes were so clear and hopeful that I didn't have the heart to tell her that my mother had hated her on sight. I couldn't tell her that black women hated "girlfriend language" when it came from white women they didn't know, and that they hated it when strangers sat on the edge of the bed where they were supposed to sleep. I didn't want to say that cancer patients don't need to hear all about dead husbands—a string of them. I didn't say that bingeing and purging stories are not appreciated by people who can't eat, but can drink little cans of strawberry-flavored chalk and water that are supposed to "Ensure" nourishment. I hugged her and patted her shoulder, and shut the door behind her.

After I saw Ginger off, I went back upstairs to talk up her virtues while Mother and I watched *Oprah*. "That was a good visit, huh?"

She wouldn't look at me. Her eyes stayed focused on the screen. "Her makeup looks pretty today," she said.

"Ginger?"

"No, Oprah. Ginger looks like a cow," Mother said.

"You know, I think after you get used to her, Ginger can probably be a big help," I said.

"No," she said. "She's not going to be a help to me. Call them and tell them that we don't need her," she said with firm conviction. "She doesn't need to come back." Her eyes were still glued to the television, but tears rolled down her cheeks. "I don't want her."

It was as if a dam had burst inside her. She became inconsolable. I offered her everything I could think of to calm her down, but I couldn't get her to stop crying. Ginger was a bit much, but I was at a loss for what she had done to cause this.

"Mama, don't cry. If she upsets you so, she doesn't have to come back. Just don't cry," I said, sitting next to her, rubbing her frail little shoulders.

She turned her head to look at me. She was so lost, helpless, but she was also angry.

"I can't do this," she said. "I just can't do it."

"Do what, Mama?"

"If I had known that they were going to cut this hole in me, I would have wished that they just let me die." There was simmering outrage in her voice.

"I can't deal with the cancer and this thing too. It's horrible. I'd rather be dead."

"No, you wouldn't," I said, but who was I to really know what she wanted at that moment?

"Yes, I would rather be dead. And that woman! She comes marching in here talking about this thing as if I just had my tonsils taken out." Her fists were balled up tight and I could see the veins in the backs of her hands pulse as she beat the bed.

"I can't . . ."

I picked my words carefully, as I did a lot these days. I didn't want to make it sound like having a colostomy and a stoma and a bag attached to your side was an everyday occurrence. It wasn't. It was a constant reminder of how bad things were. It was a billboard sign that pointed to the beginning of a loss of dignity. She couldn't do a thing about it. It had happened without her permission. All that was left was this thing that she had to learn to deal with along with chemotherapy and no appetite and no energy and no real control of the future. Nobody asked her what *she* wanted anymore. They just told her how life was going to be. It was an anger that scared me. It wasn't the same as when I got a D in high school typing, or the one time I broke curfew, or when she thought that I was rude. This was a deeper soul anger.

"You don't have to deal with it," I said and took one of her fists and put it in my hand. I took my other hand and unballed it, rubbing the palm. I looked back at her and said, "I'll do it."

"You can't do it." I felt her hand coil up again, but I wouldn't let it.

"I'll do it today. I'll do it tomorrow. I will do it next week and next year," I said. "I will do this for you until you can do it yourself."

"You'll be doing it forever then, because I will never be able to accept this awful, disgusting hole or the stupid bag I have to wear." She folded her arms around her chest.

"Let me ask you something," I said. "When I was a baby, did you ever just walk away from me and my diapers and leave me?"

She blinked. "No, of course not." Her expression softened, but only slightly.

"If I was sick, and had to have a colostomy, but I couldn't care for myself, would you leave me to get sores?"

"No, I'd take care of you," she answered without a pause.

"Exactly," I said. "I will take care of you as long as it takes, but it won't take long. I know you. When you can deal with it, you will." I got up.

She rolled her eyes and wiped her face with her wrist. "Right." She didn't believe me.

"You just have to do one thing for me. You have to let Ginger come back one more time."

"For what?"

"I need her to show me how to take care of it. Just this once. Then I'll know how. And when you feel like you are ready, I can show you."

Most reluctantly she agreed. Ginger came back, only once more, and taught me what I needed to know. And as predicted, it took only about a week before Mother was ready to start taking care of herself and be in full control. It also marked the moment when she decided that she was going to be an active participant in getting well.

"Didn't you say that the surgeon could go back in and reconnect me, if I got well?"

"Once you get well. He said that he left things in place to reconnect you, yes."

"We'll let's get busy then. I'm getting well. I'm going to get reconnected."

TEN

The following week, I started working again and Mother started inpatient chemotherapy at the hospital. We also started an unspoken ritual that would carry us through all her eight months of treatment. The night before chemo we had dinner together as a family. We planned the menus for days, with more care than most people plan Thanksgiving, Christmas, or any of the eating holidays.

The feast consisted of fried chicken, spaghetti and meat sauce, peanut butter sandwiches, McDonald's French fries, pizza, and black walnut ice cream. It was a menu of fun foods, selected based upon what sounded good to Mother and the kids. With a virtually nonexistent appetite, Mother was more fascinated by the idea of all this food spread out on the table than by the prospect of actually eating it.

"It sure looks good," she said.

Darnay and I ate, and the kids, who were picky, would eat a little chicken and spaghetti and a lot of the junk stuff. But

Mother ate only a few fries, or would get a big bowl of ice cream and dip the spoon in and lick it. Then she was done. We'd watch her, and then look at each other, then watch her some more.

I began developing a little closet cancer-related eating disorder of my own. As I cleared the table, I would eat—an extra slice of pizza here, a chicken leg there, more spaghetti with garlic bread. I was already totally full, but I would shovel food in my mouth like it was the last supper. Whenever someone came into the kitchen I'd stop, evidence that on some level I knew that this was not normal. But unlike any textbook bulimic, I didn't purge. I hung on to it. I was eating for two, Mother and me.

❧

"First we hydrate you with fluids, then antinausea medications," the nurse said. "Then we run the chemo drugs through your IV, all night."

It was the morning of the first treatment.

"That doesn't sound too bad," Mother said as she unpacked her overnight bag. They let her wear her own nightgown to make her feel more at ease. "I've got a television and a telephone. Everything I need," she said, trying to sound optimistic.

Mother decided that she wanted to be left alone at the hospital to have the chemotherapy. "I want to concentrate on my visualization," she said. She had been reading the books and listening to the tapes that the nurse at Dr. Leahy's office had given her.

She went into the bathroom to put on her gown, came back, and handed me a small white box. "Can you put my butterflies on me?"

I opened it to find about six butterfly pins of various sizes and colors. I looked at her, puzzled by their significance.

"One of the books she gave me said that you should visualize the chemotherapy as a butterfly, flying through your body, healing you." She positioned herself to sit up in the bed and prepared to be pinned. "I figure I need a lot of butterflies."

I was uneasy about leaving her alone. I was prepared to spend the day here with her so that she wouldn't be scared or lonesome. But she wanted me to go. "I have to do this part on my own. I need to focus," she said.

It made me proud to see her taking control of the process. "I'm excited about getting started. The sooner I begin, the sooner I get well." *God, I hope you're right,* I thought.

So I pinned the little butterflies all over her nightgown and kissed her on her forehead. When the nurse came back in to start the IV lines, I headed toward the door.

"You don't have to leave because of me," the nurse said. "I can do this with you here."

"No, she's afraid of needles, always has been," Mother said. And off I went to let her get about the business of being well. Focus. Focus.

While she was focusing, I went to the office to make like a gainfully employed member of society. At least that had been the intention when I went in. Mother's need for stoic concentration was very short-lived.

"Your mother is on line one," the secretary said.

Twenty minutes after we hung up, there was another buzz on the intercom. "Your mother is on line two." This went on all morning.

"Mom, do you need me to come back? I will."

"Oh, no. I really need to be still and concentrate. The book calls it 'thinking singular thoughts,'" she said.

I didn't go back, but we talked every half hour of my workday and then at home. We did this until about eight o'clock, when she and I both went to sleep. At midnight the phone rang, again.

"It burns," she said. "I feel it running through my veins. It tingles." She paused, waiting for my assessment of the situation as her own personal medical adviser. But no answer was forthcoming. It was midnight, after all. "Well, do you think that's a good sign that it's working?" she asked.

"Oh, I think so. But if you get too uncomfortable, let the nurses know."

She seemed reassured. "Okay, 'bye."

She had set down the two-day chemo rule from the first treatment. The rule was that she would go back to her apartment to be sick after her treatment. After two days, we could visit or she would come back to our house. She was expecting the worst and wanted to maintain her dignity and suffer it quietly. I respected that. But it did seem odd to have her disappear for forty-eight hours after she had become so much a part of the daily routine.

But her absences were never total, thanks to the magic of speed dial, and they allowed me something I hadn't realized that I needed until then—tiny tastes of having my own life back. For those two days, I wasn't responsible. I wasn't the daughter scrutinized by her mother. I could be worried or sad without having to mask it. I could just be me.

It was almost sensual to be able to go back to being my old sullen, moody, introspective only-child self, if just for a couple of days. Of course, our phone calls required me to step back into the role of Miss Perky, but then I could pretend that I lived hundreds of miles away. I could come up with enough idle banter to sound engaged even if I wasn't. And she never seemed to care. She just wanted the company. The two-day rule was odd, but it was a win-win proposition.

Once, during our phone calls that first day, she asked me if I understood that she needed to have that time. "Of course I do," I said, almost too enthusiastically. I did. I understood the need for solitude and privacy more than she ever had. If she hadn't been so sick, it would have been kind of amusing to see her need it, demand it. It always seemed to me that she was never particularly crazy about being alone, in her own company. But I was, and reminded her of my own little need for the two-day rule.

When I was twenty-seven, Darnay and I decided that since we had gotten through two and a half years of marriage without killing each other, we should start trying to have a baby. I didn't get pregnant that first month. Instead I got the chicken pox.

I didn't know what it was. I'd never seen it. I had been raised by a mother who was so afraid mosquito bites would kill me that, if she could help it, she made certain I wasn't around anybody contagious with anything. I was always one step short of wearing a gas mask when I was little.

Back then Darnay was working nights and I was working days. We'd talk on the phone and leave notes on the refrigerator about the important stuff. The note I left about my condition was simple.

Darnay,
    I think I have fleas. I itch all over. I have little bites. So I am going to have Kitty and Missy [our dogs] dipped this week.

                                Love,
                                Ann

He came home early one day to look at my little bites and declared that they weren't bites, but blisters. Growing up in a family of six kids, he quickly diagnosed them as the kind of blisters you get from chicken pox. I called my doctor, who over the phone confirmed my condition but definitely didn't want me to come in. I found out that I'd done all the worst things one can do, like take several long lounging baths in hopes of making the itching stop. Chicken pox does not love water. Water makes it very angry and it rewards you by spreading the blisters all over your body. And I do mean all over. I couldn't even reach the places I wanted to scratch.

Sadly, because I had never seen a living soul with chicken pox, and because everybody I talked to sort of assumed that I knew what to expect, I didn't know that the blisters eventually turn black and crusty. I woke up one morning looking like one big fat scab. And it was at this point that I invoked my version of the two-day rule: *"No, Mother, you cannot come over and tell me how terrible my scabs look."* This is now known all over the world as Andrea's Chicken Pox Rule.

She became obsessed with seeing me and my chicken pox. I became obsessed with her not seeing me and it. Stopping her became so crazy and time-consuming that for little blocks of time I forgot about the itching. She'd call. She'd show up unannounced. She'd leave because I wouldn't answer the door. She'd bribe me with all manner of stuff: "If you just let me in, I'll buy you shoes."

It wasn't long before she brought in the big guns, and my refusal to accept a bribe broke down. Ice cream was my undoing. I finally accepted. "But I'm not going to let you in," I said with determination.

She agreed without argument, convinced that I wouldn't have let her come over with it and not let her in. She had raised me better than that. But when she rang the bell, I talked to her through the peephole. "Okay. Thanks. Just put it down and go."

"No," she said. "You open this door."

I reminded her that we had a deal. "If you are going to hold me hostage over some ice cream, then take it with you. I'm not opening the door." I got back in the bed and pulled the covers over my head, but not before pulling the blinds. I knew her well enough to know that she would be creeping around the house. I was right. It wasn't long before she was tapping at my bedroom window with her keys.

"I should call the police on you, you little Peeping Tom," I shouted out to her.

Eventually she left, but there would be hell to pay later. Nonetheless, for the moment, I had pulled off a hell of a coup.

As soon as I was sure that she was really gone, I opened the door to find my rapidly melting half gallon of ice cream and a note written in eyebrow pencil: *"Here, you ignorant, ungrateful child!"*

As Mother started going through chemo, I remembered and understood her need to be able to make similar decisions. With so little under her own control, all she had was her ability to pull back when she needed to. Whether it's stage four ovarian cancer or blisters, scabs, and fever from adult-onset chicken pox, sickness sometimes demands being able to define and hold on to what you need to maintain your sense of self. Your *you*.

ELEVEN

I was glad to see her on the third day, curious, quite honestly, to see what she would look like. But she didn't look much different than she had before, except that she seemed cheerful.

"A lady came by my room while I was in the hospital," she said. "She was a cancer volunteer." She waited for my reaction. I was afraid to have one. Thinking about how she had carried on about Ginger, and how she had refused to read anything that had to do with her illness, I could only guess what she had done when this woman showed up.

"She was so nice. I liked her. She had all her hair too."

"Really?"

"She was a cancer survivor," she said. "She got breast cancer when she was fifty. Now she's sixty. About the same age as me. She volunteers her time at the hospital." She thumbed through the magazine, backward, then forward.

"A survivor, huh?" I said. "I told you. There are lots of survivors."

When I told her that she saw people at the grocery store or at the bank every day who'd survived, she thought I was making it up to make her feel better and more hopeful. And to a certain extent it was true. I couldn't find any long-term survivors who had stage four ovarian cancer.

"What did she say to you?" I asked.

She smiled and nodded slowly. "She said I can beat this, but I have to work really hard."

"Well, nobody *ever* said that to you before." As soon as I said it, I realized that I sounded a little pissed. "Didn't you and I have a donnybrook about this a month ago? Haven't I always told you that?"

"Yes. Yes you did," she said, nodding. "But *she* knew what I was going through. She's on the other side of all this."

She was right. I was saying whatever I could to get her to believe she could do it, to get her to eat and get out of bed, to make her believe that she too would be on the other side of this. But the woman Mother met had been through a double mastectomy. She'd had kick-ass chemotherapy and radiation. She was a five-year survivor who could talk to Mother about all the stuff I couldn't.

"She knew. She really knew," Mother said, smiling and crying at the same time. "She told me all about what to expect with the chemo. She told me about how she broke down when her hair fell out.

"She said that I should probably get you to cut my hair off, so that it won't be so dramatic to see it come off on a pillow or in the shower."

"She was pretty helpful, huh?"

"Yes. It's been the best thing that's happened to me since this whole mess started."

I must have gotten a really crazy look on my face, because she added, "I don't mean all the help you and Darnay have given me. I mean practical stuff. Edna calls it 'living with cancer stuff.'"

"Edna? Her name is Edna?"

"Yes. And Edna gave me some tips on how to get through it without getting so sick. She's going to bring me some books to read."

"Books?" I said, already a little jealous. "You have books. Lots of books. You won't touch them."

She twisted her mouth slightly off center, which meant that she had some profound confession on the horizon. This was going to be good. "I did look at them."

I'd just been up to the room where the stack of books was; there was a new layer of dust over them. As far as I could tell, they hadn't been disturbed.

"I looked at a couple of them. They seemed okay. I wasn't really ready to take all that in." She was watching me pace back and forth around the small apartment kitchen. "Sit down. You're making my eyes cross. I'm getting tired just looking at you."

I sat.

"I even looked at that book you carry around all the time in your purse. The one by the comic," she said.

"You read Gilda?" I read that book so much that I was on a first-name basis with Gilda Radner.

"I didn't read it. I looked at it. I read the first chapter and then I looked at the end of the book. Do you know how it ends?"

I sucked air in, realizing in that moment how stupid I had been, "Yeah, I know how it ends."

"She dies. I always look at the end of a book to decide if I want to read it. I like to know how it ends. She dies. That's the end." She looked at me as if she still just couldn't get over it. "It upset me so badly."

"And you didn't want to read about somebody who dies." I got it. I put my hands on my face, wiping some imaginary veil of insensitivity off it. "I'm sorry. I was so wrapped up in the other information in the book, that I didn't even—"

She stopped me. "Now you know why I didn't read it. You gave me more information than I needed. You gave me the information that *you* needed."

"Why didn't you tell me?" I was ashamed. Ashamed for being so mad at her for not wanting to be "informed."

"I didn't know how to tell you. You were so into it. I know you. You needed to be busy doing something."

She'd caught me. I had done all that research and gotten all those books because I felt as if I could be in control of something. "Well, you always told me that information is power," I said.

"It's too powerful sometimes. It was more than I knew what to do with. I didn't want to know how that story ends." She got up, got a soda out of the refrigerator and loaded up her glass with ice, then joined me back at the table.

"I don't know what I would do without you. I might even be dead by now," she said. "But some things you can't fix for me."

She laughed. "Remember how you used to tell me that?"

I smiled, thinking about all the times in my life that she was prepared to step in and keep me out of harm's way. "Some things can only be fixed by the person who needs the fixing," I agreed.

"So anyway, Edna was a blessing," she said, deciding that she was done talking about Gilda Radner and fixing things and me being a little busybody and her being a little busybody. "I think I'll volunteer when I get well. Maybe you're right," she said and took another sip.

"What am I right about?" I had been so wrong about the books.

"Maybe everything happens for a reason. Maybe one day I'll

get a chance to help somebody, like Edna helped me. Maybe that's why I got sick."

My words were coming back to bite me, but I nodded in agreement. "That would be great. It would make some sense out of this, huh?"

We spent the rest of the afternoon talking about Edna and her helpful hints. Because of her, Mother had decided to tell Dr. Leahy that she was ready for a venaport, which the woman in our waiting room had suggested that very first day. "She says it's much better than getting poked each and every time."

Thanks to Edna, Mother was thinking about getting well, really well. She was talking about driving and shopping and taking the kids to the zoo. She was thinking about volunteering, but not about my suggestion of a support group.

"Edna said that she had done that, and it was helpful. When I asked her if people died in the support group, she said yes." Mother got kind of weepy again. "I don't want to get attached to people and then they die. I'm afraid of that."

We agreed to take it one step at a time. When and if she wanted a support group, later, and I hoped that she did, I would find her one. I had learned my lesson well. It was really about her, and what she needed, versus what I thought she needed.

"You know what else?" she said. She had been saving the best for last, it seemed. "Edna told me that she smoked pot."

"What? What did you say?"

She nodded. "She *smoked* pot to help her with the effects of chemo. It helped her keep her weight up."

I couldn't believe that I was having this conversation with my mother. We'd never had the drug talk. It simply hadn't been necessary. I always knew what was expected of me, and was always afraid of not living up to those expectations. In college, I was so afraid of being busted, I wouldn't go in a room where other people were doing it. It would have been my luck to get hauled off to jail just for being in the same room. I didn't want to have to call back home and say, "Hey, Ma, can you get me out of jail? I got caught in a drug bust, but I wasn't smoking. Honest."

"Edna gets high? You have a pothead friend. Ooooooh," I teased. "How old is Edna? Does her mother know?" I was cracking up. "Maybe Edna is not such a good little friend for you after all." I remembered how she had said that to me about some guy I was dating in college who came to pick me up over spring break smelling like weed.

"No," she said, throwing her hands up in the air. "Edna's not some dope head who sits around all day and smokes and listens to Jamaican music and watches the Three Stooges. She did it because it helped."

Where she got this from, I had no idea, but I started laughing and couldn't stop. At first she was mad, but laughter can be infectious.

"Edna says that pot gives you the crunchies." She giggled.

"Crunchies? Oh, you mean munchies." We laughed some more.

TWELVE

Mother's laughter and confidence were short-lived. And as quickly as Edna had helped her build a fragile little foundation of hope, John took on the role of the big bad wolf and blew the house down.

She called me, almost inaudible. "He never intended to give me my car back," she said. "He thought I was going to die. He was counting on me to die."

I listened quietly, but I felt myself getting hot from the knees up. "Slow down, slow down."

"When I told him that he should start looking for a car of his own, he told me that I was rushing it. He said I wasn't ready to drive."

"When?" I asked. "When did he think you'd be ready?" It wasn't easy to hold back an opinion.

"He didn't say."

"But he gave you the keys?"

"Noooooo." She was whimpering. The rest of what she said was a mishmash of tears and anger and helplessness.

I was more puzzled than mad, although I was pretty damn pissed. Unsure about who I was madder at, him or her, I tried hard to understand why the car was an issue. If it had been me, and some man was holding my car hostage, she'd have been pouring acid on it, cutting up the tires, and breaking the windows with a baseball bat. She'd be looking for a good lawyer.

"Don't you have a set of keys too?" I asked obvious, stupid questions so that she could come up with the obvious, stupid answers all by herself. Hopefully, I could get out of this without interfering. She did have her own keys. Somehow, I knew that this was a fight I didn't want to referee. I didn't need to. Out of all the women in the world, I knew that my mother had hard-earned skills when it came to not being a victim of some man. She wasn't one to take much nonsense off anybody. She had pounded the rules of survival into my head.

I remember when she finally allowed me to have "boy phone calls" and then date; she was a relentless champion of not getting so far strung out in love or in need that you couldn't "pick your shit up and walk away." Her advice was sound, but it was so uncompromising, so inflexible, that it was difficult to negotiate the first few years of my marriage, and it was impossible to get any kind of reasonable counsel from her that would nurture marital bliss.

Now I had to listen quietly and give her advice, but on this matter I didn't have a clue as to what that was. I was a bit leery of using her own rules on her. Plus, I was about fifteen years beyond my adolescent schemes of breaking up their marriage.

"What are you going to do?" I asked as blandly as I could, trying hard to distance myself from this, although she was baiting me to defend her honor in some way.

"What can I do?" She sounded hopeless and small. I could hear her sniffling and sobbing.

I was getting weary and being pulled deeper into this latest marital melodrama. Couldn't she see that it was hard enough to be the primary caregiver? Didn't she know how afraid I was of losing her? Every day was chipping away chunks of who I had become. I couldn't be the cancer queen and Dr. Phil the marriage counselor too.

You get to learn a lot about your mother as a woman when she's sick. She's not the same person she was when she picked apart your manners or the bums that you brought home for dinner.

Even though I knew the answer, I wondered what she would have done if the tables had been turned. What would she have done if I had been sick? If I'd been the one with cancer and my husband took my car away, what would have kept her from putting a contract out on him or trying to do the job herself? Nothing. Absolutely nothing.

What kept me from doing the same on her behalf? What did she want me to do next? At any given point, she could have bounced him on his ear, but she had an unusual tolerance for him. I'm shocked to this day that she didn't send him packing after the hospital fiasco. He was still around because she wanted him there. Either she loved him, or cancer made her afraid of being alone, or she was still enchanted with the legitimacy of being somebody's wife. It really wasn't for me to judge.

I was put in the awkward position of not wanting to make anything worse. I didn't want to be responsible for tipping the balance of normalcy, whatever that was.

I decided that I would remain neutral no matter what she said. I would play the good listener, having learned that my girl-friends never really wanted my advice when it came to a bad relationship. They didn't really want me to tell them even if I knew for a fact that the guy was a homespun louse. They didn't really want me to tell them that I knew the guy screwed anything that walked and some things that didn't. They just wanted me to listen to them bitch and moan and cry. They just wanted me to know where to say "um-hmm," or "that's right," and get drunk on Long Island iced teas until nobody was fit to drive home. Even though they said, "What do you think?," they didn't really care for my opinion unless they agreed with it.

As I sat there, I tried to work this noncommittal strategy with my mother. I didn't want to throw her relationship with John back in her face. I was not going to scream, "Why are you being so goddamn stupid?" as she had done to me many times about some guy (I had, on occasion, in my single days been stuck on stupid when it came to men).

It would not have been a fair fight. It's not good to do the mother-daughter tango with someone who is chasing wastebaskets and bathrooms, throwing up every fifteen minutes, like clockwork. And after all, this was about getting her car back, not her relationship with John. To remind myself, I wrote in big block letters on a pad of paper: "IT'S ABOUT THE CAR, STUPID." I wrote it to censor myself, to keep myself cool. It was a little Zen thing I did on occasion in meetings, like Lamaze or meditation. But this time it didn't work. It just reminded me that she was being held hostage.

"Tell him to give you *your* keys," I snapped. I didn't mean to say it quite that way. It just sort of slid out. I got really quiet.

Fortunately, she was in such a tizzy about the car, she just slid right over it. "I did tell him." I could hear her blowing her nose.

"He told me that I wasn't going to get well. He said I had a black heart, and that with a heart like that, I couldn't possibly get well." She started to sob uncontrollably.

"He said what?" I needed to make sure that I'd heard her correctly before I found him and hit him in the head with a brick.

She repeated herself with such clarity that I knew she wanted me to take him on. I was being manipulated by a master in high form and I fell for it. "When did this happen?"

"When he was bringing me back from chemotherapy. I told him that I wanted the car back and that he should start looking for one of his own," she said in that tiny voice. By now, I was way past the car. If she really wanted another car, she could go out and get one that very day. He had crossed the line. She had successfully shifted their fight into a brewing hurricane between him and me.

"Where is he?" I said, gathering purse and keys. "I'm on my way."

"He's not here."

When I got to her apartment, she was running back and forth between the bathroom and the couch, loaded down with pillows and blankets.

I rolled out the plan that I had devised on my way over. "Here's what we're going to do. We're going to have a locksmith change all the locks. He has to go."

She didn't say anything, but she looked surprised that I had thought it out so quickly.

"Do you need him?" I asked. "Do you need him to make it financially?" I knew many women who, because they needed the paycheck or the benefits, have stayed with men who should have been kicked to the curb. Even though I was sure that her health benefits were covering her treatment, I figured I'd better ask.

"No. I can take care of myself."

I saw her look up behind me, and turned to find him standing there. "What's going on?" he asked.

"My mother will be needing her car back," I said. "And I am pretty sure you'll be leaving. Your presence is not helpful." I had my hands on my hips, bracing for the storm.

"What? How do you get off coming into my house and telling me where I'm going to live?" He was shouting, and looking at her. She started to cry again.

"Actually," I said, "technically the apartment is mine. The lease is in my name. And if I can't get you out of here, I will cancel the lease and take her out of here."

"What's this all about? I leave to go out to get cigarettes and I come back to you threatening to throw me out of my own house?"

"Correction, this is no threat."

It was full-out chaos from there, screaming and cursing, and she just observed us, convinced that we were fighting over her honor.

"It's okay, Ann," she said, finally.

"It's okay? You created this drama. Now it's okay?" She calmly walked toward the door and opened it. She was trying to get me to leave.

I took a deep breath. My white cotton shirt clung to me, gritty with sweat. I was out on the edge of the pier and she was pushing me off by summarily dismissing me.

"No way."

"I think you better go now," he said.

She looked at me, then at him. There were tears in her eyes. "I'm sorry. I don't feel good." Then she ran off to the bathroom. I could hear her gagging and wheezing. I turned and left.

She called an hour later, and Darnay answered the phone. "Ann, it's your mother."

"Tell her I'm asleep," I screamed. I wanted her to hear me.

"Ann, she wants to talk to you," he said, waving the phone in the air. "Don't get me in the middle of this."

I wouldn't take the call. She kept calling, and Darnay didn't want to tell her that I wouldn't come to the phone, so he just stopped answering it. "Ann, she might need you."

"No, she used me. She made me look stupid." I kept letting it ring. Finally, I figured I'd better answer in case she really was having some sort of chemo crisis.

"Yes." The responses were short.

"Hi, Baby."

"Are you okay?" I asked, voice flat-lined.

"Yes, much better," she said, trying to act as if we hadn't had civil war just hours ago. "Whatcha doing?"

"I'm busy being pissed. I have to go."

"I just can't handle being sick and dealing with this too." I couldn't figure out what part of "this" she meant. Was it the part where she played me like a fiddle, or the part where she left me hanging out to dry?

"So why the hell did you call me? You used me to beat him up. You were mad that I hadn't gone after him sooner because he wasn't doing what you thought he should. You put me in the middle of this mess. I went off like you wanted me to."

She was crying again. She was afraid, or sounded like she was. She had reason to be, knowing all along that if I had had enough, she would be left to his care. I wanted to walk away and make her feel the error of choosing his side in a fight that she had picked. I wanted her to know what it was like to be in the care of a person who told her that she had a black heart. But I knew I couldn't do it. There was too much riding on it. And everybody else knew it too.

"I'm sorry. I've just been so emotional," she said, sniffling.

I was willing to move on, but not before getting my one last question answered. "Did he really say that? That black heart stuff, did he say it?"

She was guarded now, knowing that I would go back into orbit if she said the wrong thing. But she was wrong. Once I'd figured out that I could never really walk away from all of this, then I had to find a spot that I could live with. I had to set the boundary that would keep me sane and prevent me from being caught up again. She never answered my question, and I didn't care anymore.

"I can't do this anymore," I said. "I can't fight your cancer and fight your husband too." I was calmer and more matter-of-fact than I had been since this whole thing started.

"I'll be sick too if I let you two get me caught up in your craziness. I can't sleep. I can't eat. I've been pacing around the house since I left there," I said.

"I didn't mean—"

"Yes, you did, Mother. But you didn't think it would get that ugly," I said. "You didn't think I would go that far. You used me to beat him up because you didn't have the strength or inclination to do it yourself."

She didn't say a word.

"Are you going to stay married to him? Is he going to stay there?" I asked. I already knew the answer from the pause.

"Okay, new plan," I said, presenting my terms, the only ones I would accept. "You are not ever going to tell me another negative thing about your husband. I don't care what he says or what he does." I pictured him making her walk to her chemo appointments. "I don't want to hear another peep."

"That's not fair." My mother, who hated whining, was mewing at me.

"No, Mom. What's not fair is that you stir me up to protect you. You don't need protecting. You are going to get over this thing with him and think he should be able to come to my house for Sunday dinner. You are going to want us all to hold hands and sing Christmas carols around the tree or 'Kumbaya' or some stupid shit like that. You are going to want me to make small talk."

"But—"

"I can't do that if you keep this up. So here is the deal. Not a negative word about him to me or in my presence. If you want to bitch about him, call Auntie Gloria or Gussie or Frances. Not me."

"Okay," she said, grateful that I hadn't asked her to choose between the two of us again.

"And you are going to tell him that he better not ever get an attitude with me. You better fix that, or I will leave the two of you to your own dysfunctional devices." I hung up the phone and went to bed with a migraine.

The next morning, she called early and we picked up like the day from hell had never happened.

THIRTEEN

About three weeks later, Mother's hair fell out in fuzzy chunks, just as we knew it would. I was actually relieved because I had worried that if the chemotherapy didn't make her hair fall out, maybe it wasn't strong enough, but I didn't know how to say that to her. But her reaction to her hair loss caught me by surprise. She cried.

We had talked about this before and decided that it was going to be easier for her than for most women, because she was already wearing wigs. She had for years. "So, what's another wig? No big deal." But it was a big deal, big enough that I had to leave work to go calm her down.

On the way to her house, I stopped and picked out some beautiful silk scarves to cheer her up. I thought about the importance that hair played in a woman's identity, I thought about how my mother reacted every time she saw my haircut.

"If you're going to wear it like that, you better keep a good hairdresser and go every week," she'd say. "Or if you get tired of that . . . look, then you could always get a wig."

"Or I could get braids, or dreads, or just let it be natural," I'd say to get a rise out of her. "I was thinking about some dreads."

When I got there, she was sitting on a rug in the middle of the living room floor, surrounded by small, fluffy piles of her natural hair. It had been so long since I'd seen it, that I'd forgotten that it was once brown and soft and curly. I kneeled down next to her. "I bought you something. Let's put one on." I carefully smoothed down her remaining hair, and tied one of the scarves kerchief style. "There."

"Maybe I should just get the clippers and shear it off," she said as she reached under the scarf and pulled out more patches of hair, studying them before laying them next to the others. She was looking at the hair with such amazement that it made me wonder what she was thinking. She was mourning something that had never had much value for her, as far as I knew.

"I remember that you used to look like Diana Ross with those wigs," I said.

She had been the most glamorous person I'd ever seen. When I was five or six, she was in her ash-blonde flip days. She used to punctuate the look with a drawn-on beauty mark, as if to say, That's all, that's it. But that wasn't all. There were *the* clothes. She wore movie-star clothes. Jackie Kennedy suits. Dorothy Dandridge cocktail dresses. The Supremes. Oh, she was something.

When I went to middle school in the late sixties, other mothers had press and curls, or Afros. I had grown to hate the wigs, and she was always a little too much to fit in with the other mothers. The wigs just got darker and shorter, but they never went away. She changed them like she changed outfits, never seeming to give much thought or care to her own hair, short of washing and combing it.

"I guess what they say is true," she said, and finally looked up at me.

"What's that?"

"Use it or lose it." She smiled. Then she giggled, picking up a ball of hair.

"I have an idea," I said. "When the going gets rough, the rough go . . . wig shopping." Finally I was able to convince her to get rid of the new gray ones that made her look like Harpo Marx.

FOURTEEN

We'd been anxious for the chemotherapy to begin, but over the months of treatment, short of the fact that she was now bald as an egg, nothing happened. Nothing you could see anyway. I never saw big changes and said, "Yeah, now you're cooking." But it didn't stop me from looking daily for little signs and signals. There weren't many.

For the observer, no matter how close, chemotherapy is like a really good thriller. You have to hang in there. You keep watching and waiting and you don't know how it ends, until it does. There are no real clues as to how it's working. The outcome is all guesswork until the very last page.

However, there were some signs that her confidence was coming back, and that she needed to be in control again. After the first months of treatments, she wrested her car keys back along with her independence. Once she felt up to driving, she started venturing out a little bit every day. Usually she went to the mall, or the video store, or the grocery store, armed with the newspaper sale pages.

When she went out, she didn't eat much, though she and John

were particularly fond of the "all-you-can-eat" places in town. Most of her time was spent driving back and forth to my house on a daily basis. Her weekends were almost always spent with us.

She had monthly checkups with Dr. Leahy. Blood counts up. Blood counts down. Weight up. Weight down. Let's order a transfusion. Doing great. See you next month. It was like being in suspended animation. Life kept its day-to-day pace, but the future was on hold. Some days it hurt to breathe, or smile, or think about what was coming next. It was all speculation, like tap dancing on thin, early-winter ice.

Gradually, I could see bright shiny things happen. At about four months into her treatment, Mother seemed to turn a corner. Chemo still knocked her out, and her hair was still missing in action, but she was rebounding a little at a time. Every new thing that she was able to do amazed and amused her. Walking to the mailbox, doing laundry, cooking a whole meal, staying out longer than an hour were joys that she hadn't expected to have in her life again. She felt blessed and renewed: "I thought I'd never be me again."

I felt grateful too. There were still no concrete signs that the cancer was going away, but there were no signs that it wasn't, either. Each day, as she gained more of her independence, she gained more hope that was all her own. She wasn't believing that she'd get well just because I wanted her to believe it. She was believing it because she was getting stronger and able to do more every day.

By month six, she was eating almost normally, which meant that I could stop eating for two. I loved to see her eat, for her sake and for mine.

Once she felt that she was looking and feeling better, she decided to go back to Gary for a visit, but she was intent on keeping her secret. She told no one that she had cancer, or that she was in the middle of heavy-duty chemotherapy, and insisted that we keep her secret too.

FIFTEEN

As Mother's treatments continued, the costume jewelry butterflies still seemed to work well for her, but the imaging tapes got old fast. So I made a bunch of tapes of her favorite singers for her to listen to at her next chemo session. She'd never been a huge music person, at least not in the way that Darnay and I were. We had hundreds of CDs, everything from Miles Davis to Parliament and Funkadelic and Bob Marley. I even had a collection of Streisand and a pile of show tunes, and, of course, some Duke Ellington and Louis Armstrong.

But Mother was a music loyalist. She had a handful of favorites and she held them dear: Nancy Wilson, Dinah Washington, Nat King Cole, and Arthur Prysock. She liked what she liked, and I found out that being sick didn't do much to broaden her horizons. I put together a stack of cassettes with artists that I thought would make her happy, went through these for her to see which ones she wanted to take with her to the hospital the next morning.

"Billie Holiday? I saw her once at a little club on the South Side," she said as she lounged on the couch in her apartment. I suddenly saw her in a new, more interesting light. Who knew? My mother had been in a room with someone as famous as that and had never said a word about it, at least that I could remember. Maybe she had when I was fifteen and thought that she and her music were Stone Aged compared to Marvin Gaye. Maybe she said it and I just didn't want to hear her.

I closed my eyes and tried to picture my mother with a fresh hairdo, all dolled up in a fancy silk or satin dress, sitting with the Girlfriends or some good-looking guy in a snappy sharkskin suit, smoking a cigarette, sipping a drink, swaying to "No Regrets."

"No. She wasn't such a big deal by then. She wasn't on her game anymore. It was shortly before she died. She wore these long gowns," my mother said, looking through the stack of cassettes. "You know why?"

"Why?"

"Because she ran out of places to shoot up. There were needle marks around her ankles."

Lady Day's voice was gone from too much dope, too much booze, too many smoky rooms. Mother said she drew crowds because she was Billie Holiday more than because she could still sing. "It was pitiful to see. She could hardly keep her eyes open. It was like she was singing to herself," Mother said. "When you think about it, she had the saddest music that you'd ever want to hear. Makes me want to cry, sitting here talking about it." She put the cassette aside. "Take this one back. It's too sad to listen to when you're having chemo."

She asked what else I had in the stack. I had some Aretha Franklin, a little Gladys Knight. Some Temptations. "That's your stuff," she said, shaking her head. "You got some Sweet Nancy in there?"

I smiled. Of course I did. I had old Nancy Wilson cuts and some from the newer albums. She didn't want the new ones. It was the old songs that held the magic and the elegance that would take her mind off what was going on. "Why don't I put this one on," I said, and played, "Guess Who I Saw Today," which was my mother's all-time favorite song.

It was more like a story, a little soap opera. In the song, Nancy meets her husband at the door with a martini and carefully details the ins and outs of her very ordinary day. You could just picture this very stylish, beautiful woman, showstopping in her ladies-who-do-lunch suit, matching pumps, and gloves, and her perfectly bouffant hairdo. She looks straight out of a Doris Day movie. She stops in this little café to get out of the rain. Sitting in a booth, she is struck by a couple sitting across the room. They're so much in love, Nancy tells us. She whispers, as if she's telling a little secret. They are so wrapped up in each other that they don't see her or anybody else. She goes on about her leisurely afternoon, dropping bits and pieces of what she saw until she closes in for the kill. "Guess who I saw today, my dear?"

It is the kind of song that if you've heard it more than once, you can't help but sing along and act it out. That's what Mother and I did less than eight hours before she went back into the hospital. We sang "Guess who I saw today, my dear?" and we pointed our fingers at the imaginary husband. We took long drags off the invisible cigarette that you had to have if you were going to be really glamorous, and pulled it away from our lips Bette Davis style. We shook our heads and put our hands on our hips the way that black women do when we are getting ready to screw you up. Hold on, baby, it's going to be a bumpy ride.

"Guess who I saw? Guess who I saw? Guess. Who. I. Saw?" we sang loud, getting ready for the big finish. "I . . . saw . . .

you!" We laughed, and fell on the floor and clapped. She could forget about cancer while she listened to Nancy front her man off about his affair in such a ladylike manner.

And please, honey! You have never heard "Teach Me Tonight" until you've heard it performed by Dinah Washington with my mother and me singing backup. "Should the teacher stand so near, my love. Graduation's almost here, my love. Teach me, tonight." How many Saturday nights did I get my hair washed, detangled, braided, dried, and hot combed to Dinah's music?

I always thought Etta James had the same heady qualities as Dinah Washington, and added her the stack. But when I put on one of her CDs, Mother wrinkled up her nose as if she was smelling feet or armpits. "Oh, no. Not her."

"What's wrong with Etta? I like her."

"Too common," she pronounced. "Common."

My mother had never been into blues, which she viewed as "common." She liked her music "classy."

"I prefer my music to sound like it's served with champagne instead of Colt 45 or Mad Dog," she said. So we sent her off the next morning armed with a box of classy chemo music.

SIXTEEN

On November 22, Mother and I began preparing for the biggest and best holiday ever known to the world. Later that day, we were going grocery shopping for the three families we had "adopted" for Thanksgiving. Darnay left for work, Nicole was at school, and Christopher was watching cartoons in his room. We were still in our pajamas, making lists and watching the *Today Show* coverage of the Kennedy assassination anniversary.

"Ann, I don't want to be a vegetable," she said out of the blue.

I looked over, confused. Where did she come up with that? "What did I miss?"

"I was just remembering," she said. "When Kennedy got shot, at first they didn't know if he'd make it or not. At least that's what they were saying." She took a long sip of her morning cola. "They said that if he survived, he would always be a vegetable. You probably don't remember that."

I did remember. I was just in the second grade, but it was the most dramatic and tragic thing that would ever happen to us, all of us. The event has been imprinted on us through books and anniversary shows and interviews like the ones we were watching that morning.

"I couldn't stand to be like that . . . a vegetable."

Since cancer hit, some days we went from big, panoramic highs, lots of energy, plans, and festivities to hitting the wall, hard. It happened without any warning. Anything could trigger it. Some days I was better at talking about cancer than others. Today was not a good day.

I wanted to get her off the subject, so I changed the channel, but even the home-shopping channels were selling commemorative coins and Jackie O dolls.

So I said, "I could be a vegetable, if I thought about it. Asparagus. Asparagus wouldn't be bad. I like asparagus now. Just as long as I didn't have to turn into okra. Greens wouldn't be good either." I thought it was pretty clever, under the circumstances.

She cut her eyes sharply in my direction. "You are so damn funny," she said, giving me one of those eagle-chasing-a-farm-animal looks. "I'm serious. I'm trying to tell you something important to me." She was tapping the table to emphasize the importance of what she wanted to say. "If I ever get that bad, you have to promise that you won't let me be a . . . vegetable."

I switched back to *Good Morning America*. There were the old photos of Jackie in that pink suit, one with the matching hat, splattered with her husband's blood. One look at the suit and the abject horror on her face should have told anybody that he wouldn't survive. He was never going to be a vegetable. My heart hurt for her, even now. And it hurt for my mother, who associated every tragedy, from the Kennedy assassination to the kidnapping of the Lindbergh baby, with her own illness.

"Ma, what does what happened to President Kennedy really have to do with you, anyway?" I left the room to get some juice and came back. It was about eight o'clock in the morning, but this conversation had me thinking it was midnight. "He got shot in the head. He didn't have cancer. Cancer patients don't usually turn into turnips," I said. "You think?"

She didn't like the way that I was responding. "Stupid. You can act so stupid," she said. "Shows what you know." She cited some person she knew from the old days in Gary, my fourth-grade teacher. "He had cancer. They say he hardly knew his own kids at the end. Couldn't feed himself. Just sat there and cried all day." She nodded at me. She had proved her point as far as she was concerned. "A vegetable."

She hadn't proved a thing to me with that example. "That bastard was a vegetable long before he got cancer. He was a prune."

"You are so mean."

I'd had enough. "Ma, get over it. Kennedy has been dead most of my adult life. Just because somebody four hundred years ago said that if he lived, he was going to be a damn eggplant, you decide that your fate is ever entwined with his. What the hell is that?" I threw my hands up in the air with such force that I lost my balance and fell back.

"I just worry, that's all. You just have to help me make sure that it doesn't happen."

It was the first time that we had discussed anything like this. What was I supposed to do if she ever got to the point where things went really bad? What was she telling me? What was she expecting from me now? This was much too serious for somebody who was supposed to go out that very afternoon and buy turkeys and sweet potatoes and deliver baskets to people who were down on their luck.

"Okay, okay. I promise. Let's just stop talking about it," I said, not knowing what I was really promising to do. "If you start getting broccolilike, or sprouting extra eyes like a damn potato, I will put you out of your misery and cook you up with a nice cheese sauce. Is that okay with you?" I went upstairs to take a shower, propped myself up against the tiles, and cried.

SEVENTEEN

If Thanksgiving was any indication, Christmas was going to be an over-the-top production. It always had been, and this year we were operating with the ghost of Christmas Future peering over our shoulders. Mother was rebounding well and putting on weight. She sailed through the early December chemo treatment. I should have been able to relax a bit, but I wouldn't let my mind think that everything was going to be okay.

Some days, moments like when we decorated the tree, or sat around the living room watching the Grinch, or the Charlie Brown Christmas show with its beautiful, joyfully sad music, I caught a glimpse of her in the glow of the blinking, twinkling lights, and got so weepy sad that I had to leave the room "to get more eggnog." There was an unspoken buzz, but clearly felt by all. This could be the last Christmas that we would all be together. The very last one.

And so we set out to re-create one of those perfectly excessive Christmas scenes that I had loved when I was a little girl, but grew embarrassed by when I became an adolescent, and was mortified by when I hit high school. It's no wonder that so many people kill themselves during the holidays. The unmet expectation of perfection in gifts, food, carolers, parties, love, and familial goodwill are enough to make you long to be one of the chestnuts roasting on an open fire just to be put out of your misery.

> Dear Santa,
>> Please shoot me now.
>>> Love,
>>>> Me
>
> P.S.
> Bah, humbug.

There would be no humbug allowed this Christmas. We revived old traditions from my childhood and continued the ones that Darnay and I had started together. After Nicole was born, he and I had a family portrait taken during the holidays.

This year we included Mother, and instead of having the picture taken at Sears, I asked a friend who was a top-notch portrait and wedding photographer to come to the house. Darnay and Christopher were all suited up, Nicole was in a holiday dress with a silk plaid skirt and patent leather shoes that my mother had bought her, and I wore one of the black knit dresses that she had given me for Christmas every year since I'd turned eighteen. "You can never have enough basic black," she said. None of her own dress clothes fit her, so she wore a red dress that I'd bought in a sample sale and couldn't get into since I'd started eating hell off hinges.

We were the picture-perfect Huxtable family. But when the proofs came back, I saw something in my mother's eyes that I hadn't seen the day they were taken. She had a look of contentment and satisfaction that was stunning given what she was going through.

Mother, father, children, perfect house, perfect tree, everybody loved each other. She was sitting in the middle of one of her fantasies. She'd gotten what she had wanted her whole adult life. She belonged to a family like the ones on television. She'd always wanted a middle-class, English Tudor life, with a mother and a father and kids wrapped up in a neat bundle.

In her own effort at re-creating her ideal life, she had gotten the house, and she came with a kid, but she, John, and I were never like the young family in the Christmas picture. In fact, there were almost no photos that documented the three of us as any kind of family. In the only one I can remember, she is standing sandwiched between the two of us, cheesing from ear to ear, as if she's won some wonderful prize. John and I were both there under protest, he looking like his feet hurt, and I, with a face full of oily-skin acne, being pinched into submission. It said everything about what our household was like on a daily basis.

I heaped other presents on her that Christmas, but it was the picture, and what it represented to her, that was the hit of the holidays. She presented me with a list of people that she wanted to make sure got a copy of "me and my family," to show that she had gotten what she'd set out to have after all.

John wasn't in the picture, although I offered. "That won't be necessary," she said. "He's going to be gone. I told him that he should spend the holidays with his family." When I look at the picture, it is like someone took a pair of embroidery scissors and skillfully cut him out.

He stayed gone until after the first of the year, traveling as a roadie for an up-and-coming boxer from Lansing. He'd made a choice. "I'm not missing him, are you?" she said.

Instead she put all her energies into re-creating the Christmases of my childhood, when there had been so much stuff under the tree that I never got around to opening it all. Sometimes I thought it was overcompensation for being a single parent or guilt because she worked outside the home. There were times when I was sure that it came from being a child of the Depression; she wanted me to have everything she'd never had. It was great, but it also got me so excited that I threw up every single Christmas. She had always judged the success of the day by how sick I got. As I got older and stopped being sick, she lost a bit of her Christmas glow.

She regained it with a fervor when Nicole and Christopher came along. This year, between the gifts she distributed on Christmas Eve, and the things that Santa, Darnay, and I brought out on Christmas Day, there was no clear spot on the floor.

It was, of course, too much for two little children to wrap themselves around. "I didn't think we were that good," Nicole told me in confidence.

"You weren't. Granny paid Santa off," I said, providing a perfectly acceptable reason to Nicole. Chris didn't care where it all came from, he was just glad it was there.

Later, after hours of gift exchange and serious play, after turkey and dressing and sweet potatoes and fried corn, after potato salad and seven-layer salad, after moaning and groaning and belt loosening, Mother was worried.

"What's wrong with you?"

"I'm not sure they had a good time," Mother said. "I wanted this to be so special."

I looked around the living room. "It's a toy supermarket in here."

"But they didn't get sick. You would always have to go sit on the side of the tub."

"I was fragile. Plus, the night is young. With all that food we ate, somebody is going to get sick before it's over. It might be you or me, but it will happen."

She wasn't convinced. At eight o'clock the next morning, which was my birthday, she went out trolling the after-Christmas sales for more stuff. "Happy birthday, Baby."

I opened my gifts and took my cue. I perched myself on the side of the tub with a cold washcloth pressed to my face.

"Now it feels like Christmas," she said, satisfied.

EIGHTEEN

After the excess of the holidays, she came in one day with yet another surprise. "Look what I found," she said as she presented me with a big grocery sack, its contents spilling out.

It didn't take much digging to see that she had just handed me a treasure chest of memories. She had found my Barbies.

"There's another whole box in the back of the car. You're lucky that they didn't get thrown away in the move to Las Vegas."

I carefully took the dolls out of the bag, one by one, rejoicing at the sight of each one. I hadn't seen this stuff in twenty years. They had been my best friends; as I was often a lonely only child, some days they were my only friends.

"They all look just like new," I squealed. "Look at these outfits. They look like they were bought yesterday." I held up little gold lamé sheaths and tiny straw hats. Each outfit, each doll, had its own story. I remembered how each one had come into my possession.

"Look, Ma, here's a Bubble Cut. This one's Tutti, Barbie's baby sister." Then I held up Midge. I had never liked Midge much. She was sort of homely, with big bug eyes and a goofy grin. But every girl needed a buddy; Barbie had Midge. And now, in my needy little hands, I had them both.

"So, are you going to give all this stuff to Nicky?"

"No way. This is my stuff. There ain't no way that I'm giving them up. Have you seen the Barbies she has? Most of them don't even have heads anymore."

"What are you going to do with them?" she asked, in disbelief.

"I'm going to play with them. Then, who knows? I might sell them. They pay a lot of money for vintage Barbies and clothes in mint condition."

"You used to love those dolls. I could hardly get you to do your homework. I never understood what you saw in them." She picked one up, frowned at it, and put it back down. "Baby dolls. They were better. I liked baby dolls." My mother had always seemed to crave the things she didn't have growing up.

For every single Barbie I asked for and got at Christmas, I also got three round-headed, pudgy-legged baby dolls that I hadn't asked for and had no interest in playing with once they arrived with their assorted layettes, beds, high chairs, bathtubs, and wardrobes.

"Remember that one doll you bought me? The one with bad breath?" I asked.

She nodded. It was one of those big, oversize baby dolls that said "Mama" when you squeezed its soft belly. It had a rubberized stomach and you got a whiff of rubber-band breath when you squeezed it. "You didn't like her," Mother said. But I remembered that she had liked it a lot.

"What about Thumbelina? You killed her on Christmas." My mother murdered one of my dolls on Christmas Day. Not on purpose. It was involuntary babydollicide, I suppose.

Thumbelina had a knob in her back that allowed her to roll around, back and forward, "like a real baby". She was another doll that I hadn't asked for and hadn't wanted. Good thing too. I couldn't get within an inch of her anyway. From the time she came out of her box until her untimely demise, she was Mother's constant Christmas companion. Mother cooed and twisted her knob and watched her roll around so often that the poor doll just gave up and died. Dead as a doorknob.

Mother was horrified that she had broken it. "I'm so sorry," she said over and over again, as if I cared. "I'll get you another one tomorrow," she promised. But I didn't want another one. I thought Thumbelina was freak-show scary. And I found it creepy that my mother was so taken with her.

"If you're going to replace her, can we get a black-haired Barbie instead?" So I got a black-haired Barbie, *and* a new Thumbelina who met the same unfortunate fate as the first one. My mother, the baby-doll killer.

❧

A month later, after many phone calls tracking down leads, I found Betty, an older lady who was the big doll collector in town. She had dolls from as far back as the Civil War, but like me, she had a special passion for the Barbies.

On one of the nights that Mother was having chemo, Betty invited me over for coffee. "Bring your stuff. Let's have a look," she said.

I was looking forward to getting out of the house to talk to someone, anyone, about something other than cancer and doctors and treatments. It was a play date. But I, armed with all my dolls, was surprised when Betty opened the door. Betty's face was all twisted and malformed, from a stroke, I guessed.

"I have cancer. Bone cancer in my face. I've had reconstructive surgery a couple of times, but the cancer just keeps eating away at everything they try to do." There was no self-consciousness to her statement. It was just a matter of fact. "I'm almost eighty years old. I'm not trying to get a man, and I'm not going to be Miss Michigan anytime soon. So the hell with it."

"My mother has cancer too," I said, looking past her deformities and into her eyes.

With that uncomfortable moment behind us, we settled in for some serious doll talk and play. She pulled out her reference book and helped me inventory what I had.

"Oh my. You have some things I've never even seen in person. Just in books. This is a fine collection indeed."

I was proud. I explained that I was able to keep the clothes in such good shape because when I was little, my mother let me have them dry-cleaned in little sweater bags when we went to the self-serve dry cleaners on Saturdays.

She smiled sadly, as if she felt sorry for me. She looked at me in the way that people look at orphans. I couldn't be mad. I was sure that I was looking at her the way that other people looked at her too. Misfits playing dolls. What could be more satisfying? "I'll offer you three thousand dollars for the lot," she said. "But here's what I'd do if I were you." She was combing Francie's hair with a tiny brush.

"I'd go out and get a price book. Then go to a couple of Barbie shows to see what they're selling for."

I had no idea that there was such a thing as a Barbie show, with hundreds of vendors selling Barbie cars, mansions, dogs, coats, earrings, and the rarest of dolls. It made my little shopper's heart skip a beat.

"Don't sell anything until you do that. Then join the Barbie Club here, if you'd like."

"I can't join anything right now, with the kids being little and . . ."

"With your mother being sick?" she guessed.

I nodded as tears flooded my eyes. This moment with Betty was the closest I was going to be able to come to having an outside buddy for a long, long time and I knew it.

"Did you love your Barbies when you were little, honey?"

She had no idea. I loved them so much that it hurt to let her touch them and play with their clothes now. "Yes. I loved them a whole lot."

She sat thoughtfully, looking at me, then back at the dolls. "Well, then, let me make another suggestion."

I listened intently while I rubbed my fingers across the red velvet of my favorite outfit.

"Keep 'em. Play with 'em," she said. "When I was having treatment, it made me feel better to play with my dolls. If you loved them, the way I see in your eyes, it might make you feel better somehow too."

Once I decided that I would keep them, it did make me feel better. It put me back in that position of being a little girl who had something that she treasured. It made me feel safe again. I thought about what Betty had said, and stopped at the toy store on the way home and bought the closest thing I could find to a Thumbelina for my mother. Maybe it would make her feel better too.

It wasn't long before I was sending off for catalogs and subscribing to *Barbie Bazaar*. The next thing you know, I was adding to my collection, filling in things I didn't have or that had been lost or stolen by neighborhood kids. It was calming and weird to be doing this in the midst of trips to the oncologists and the pharmacist. Everything around me seemed so shaky that having this part of my past here put me instantly into a time where all was right with my world. It was like thumb sucking, to calm myself down after a bad day. There would be a lot of Barbie thumb sucking, because in between some really good days, we were headed for some rough ones. And on each one of them, I would go running to my treasure chest.

NINETEEN

As I found comfort in little dolls in high heels, my mother and children found comfort in other ways. Some parents tell bedtime stories about fairies and gingerbread children, heroes and dragons. Not me. While she was undergoing treatment, she forced me to tell her and the children the story of her uncle Marcel, who as a young man was living alone in the big city when he fell desperately ill. He was sure he was going to die.

Though I can't remember what his real ailment had been, he was, by the admission of every family storyteller, one sick puppy. His situation was made even more pitiful because he had no friends or relatives to help him.

"And then what happened?" Ma said, eyes wide open as if she had not heard this story three thousand and three times before.

"Well, then Nanny comes to visit," I said. Nanny Strickland was my mother's grandmother, a formidable woman at four-eleven, who was part black, part white, and part Native American. Her mother had been a freed slave.

"But Nanny is dead," Nicole chimed in. Both the children were sitting cross-legged on the floor, bathed and ready for bed. Mother sat on her bed in her pink flannel nightgown, her head wrapped in a terry-cloth turban.

"Okay, yeah, Nanny is dead." This was the punch line of the story. This was the favorite bedtime tale, for some reason, and everybody, including baby Christopher, knew it was a "true" family ghost story.

I continued. "Nanny shows up with a suitcase, and unpacks to stay a spell."

"What's in the suitcase?" Ma asked even though she knew the story by heart.

I rolled my eyes. "Okay, okay. The suitcase. I don't really know why a dead woman needs a suitcase, but she has one. She's a ghost. She's dead and she comes in dragging a suitcase."

Nicole raised her hand to ask a question, like they were taught in school.

"Nicole?"

"Doesn't Uncle Marcel know she's dead? He has to know she's a ghost. She is his mother, after all. Wouldn't he know if she's dead?"

I didn't have the answer to this. Plus, logic always broke the timing of the telling of the story. Christopher saved me. "Shhhh, let Mommy tell."

"What's in the suitcase?" my mother asked.

"Ghost stuff. You know. Ghost girdles and bras. Ghost pillows and blankets. Dresses, soap."

"Diapers?" Christopher asked. "Milk?"

"Aren't all of you sleepy yet?" I just wanted to be done with the story. I had already told it three times this week.

"No, please. Finish. We'll go to sleep after you finish," Ma said.

"Okay. Where was I? Yeah, I know. She had lotion in there too. Ghosts get really dry skin. That's why they always look so white."

They laughed. They loved that part. "What about books?" Nicole said. She was jumping ahead.

"Yes, there were books. Because she needed something to do while Uncle Marcel was resting. So she had ghost books. You know: *Dark Shadows, The Ghost and Mrs. Muir, Topper, The Legend of Sleepy Hollow.*

"But she didn't take any time away from Uncle Marcel. She took really good care of him. She mixed herbs and tonics and brews to make him well."

"He had a fever?" Ma said.

"Yes. And when the fever broke, Marcel woke up."

"And Nanny was gone," they all chimed in.

"Yes," I said. "She was gone as quickly as she had arrived."

They wanted to know what happened to the suitcase. They wanted to know how she made him well. They wanted to know where she went. But for me, the story was over.

"When she made him well, she went back to heaven with her suitcase. That's all. The end. Now let's all hit the sack."

My mother loved this fractured, family fairy tale even more than the kids did. While she was undergoing treatments, I had to tell it at least once a week. Sometimes she would call from the hospital and I'd excuse myself from meetings to whisper it to her so she could go back to sleep. It didn't matter that the original teller of the tale, Uncle Marcel, was a diagnosed schizophrenic who throughout his life saw ghosts, or devils, or talking dogs. Every family has a crazy uncle; he was ours. Who knew that his little story would give her hope to hang on to all these years later? The story came to be much more about my mother and her own mother than it was about Uncle Marcel and Nanny Strickland, anyway. I think Mother waited patiently every day for my grandmother to march in and make the cancer go away.

"Have you seen her lately?" she'd ask hopefully.

"Nanny? You know I've never seen Nanny. She's been dead for sixty years. I wouldn't know her anyway." I knew she didn't mean Nanny. She wanted to know if I had felt the presence of her mother in the house, which I have been known to do on many occasions. I've fallen asleep and gotten up with a sense of calm and smelled her citrusy-sweet hair pomade all around me. There have been times when I was sure that she had her arms around me. And when both my children were born, I felt her in the room with me the night before I went into labor.

This never sat well with my mother. "Why does she talk to you, and not to me?"

The answer, as I saw it, was simple. I let her talk to me. I listened. Yet I hadn't felt her presence much since we'd started this cancer journey. I think this happened for the same reason that my mother never felt her. I stopped listening. I stopped being still. The few times I had felt her share things with me about my mother's condition, they weren't positive. So I had turned the sensors off. I still needed to believe.

Mother still needed to believe too, so on days when she was depressed because the chemo had turned her insides out, or when her bones ached, I'd say, "Grandma was here. It's gonna be okay." I was amazed by what a skilled liar I had become.

"Do you think if you asked her, she would tell you what's going to happen?" she asked.

"Ma, I don't think it works that way. I'm not the Psychic Friend."

This would make her even sadder. Her own mother didn't seem to be coming to her rescue. Or I wasn't cooperating as a helpful medium. So one day when she was feeling particularly good, she came to pick up Nicole to take her to Toys "R" Us and spend the night at her place.

Two days later, I got a call from the school and found out

that they had bought a Ouija board at the store. Nicole had brought it in for sharing, and her teacher was freaked out.

When I asked Nicole about it, she said, "Granny bought it. She said that we could talk to Grandma Lucille. She said you wouldn't be happy, so we couldn't tell."

I went over to my mother's place with fire in my eyes. "Nicole almost got kicked out of school today for being a witch. This is not good."

"I just wanted to—"

As I looked at her, I could see how abandoned and lost she felt. I couldn't stay mad at her. "I told you, I don't think it works that way. And if she thinks you are trying to conjure her up on some $7.99 Ouija board, she could just go away. So you have to stop it."

She started to cry. "I didn't mean to get Nicky in trouble. I just—"

"Well, let me tell you something that I do know. Grandma might not come busting in here with a steamer trunk, and we know that's the only way she could get all her stuff anywhere. But I know that she stays close by you."

Her face was cautiously optimistic. "I've never seen her or smelled her like you do."

"She's here a lot. I know it. There's no way that she would let you go through this alone. Plus," I smiled, "everybody knows that I'm not responsible enough to handle such a big job by myself. Ma, I know she has her eyes on you. She's with you every step of the way."

She wiped her eyes, and her color seemed to come back. "Do you really think so? You're not just saying that?"

I winked. "I know so."

TWENTY

Time flew by. Next thing I knew eight months had passed and we had an appointment with the oncologist to go over the results of the chemotherapy. If the test results looked good, she would schedule a CAT scan. We were entering a whole new phase of this odyssey. The weight of it made it impossible to sleep.

I was up at four-thirty that morning, wanting to soak in the quiet that is only available that early in the day. I needed to meditate, to pray, and to summon up my courage. After all the chemo, this was it. This was the day we would find out if it had worked. I sat in the rocking chair with eyes closed and heart open, focusing on my intuition, trying to pick up the slightest sign of what the doctor would have to say.

In the deepest part of my heart, I was expecting—no, bracing for—the worst. On the surface, I acted confident that we were going to get good news. But here in the dark of my living room, I was truly fearful. I tried to picture her at her place, hoping that she was sleeping soundly. But I knew that if I called her, she would be wide awake too, steadying herself, asking God to give her the strength to accept whatever was ahead.

I would have cried, but I was afraid that I wouldn't be able to turn it off. There had been so many moments when I'd wanted to come apart at the seams, stitch by stitch, but I knew that was a luxury that I couldn't afford. Sitting here in the stillness, waiting for results, the beginning of this journey seemed so far away. Eight months ago seemed like eight years. I felt older. I had become a very, very responsible adult.

Eventually the silence was broken by a phone call from Mother. "You awake?"

"Yes, Ma. Are you?" I said and laughed.

"What time are you coming?" she asked.

"Well, since it's five-thirty now, I'm thinking if I leave in four hours, it takes me five minutes to get to you, I should be there at nine thirty-five," I said, a little smile in my voice.

"You are ignorant," she said and hung up.

I didn't walk away from the phone because I knew . . .

"Hello, Ma. What now?"

"What are we going to have for dinner today?"

Between calls like that about every fifteen minutes and children who needed their faces washed and breakfasts made, and a husband who couldn't figure out if his shirt was gray or green, the morning was filled with noise and clutter.

As promised, I was at her apartment at 9:35 A.M., and to my surprise, she was standing in the parking lot waiting for me. God help me if I had been late.

We sat in the same room, oddly enough with some of the same people from the very first office visit. Or maybe they weren't. After going to so many office visits with my mother, I was convinced that all cancer patients looked like that. Patches on eyes, scars the size of railroad tracks, walkers, amputated legs, bald heads. They looked the same as that first day, but much smaller, shrunken, melted-down versions of their former selves. I noticed that one of the regulars was missing in action. Anytime one of the cancer-crew regulars doesn't show up, it gives you pause. Did he have a setback? Did she die since the last time? A couple of regulars did die in those eight months.

I now understood why Mother had been so adamant about not wanting to join any kind of support group even though I pushed it. "I don't want to have to worry about other people dying," she'd said. Minutes away from hearing the most important news since this awful thing had happened, I was worried about other people dying. Even though I hadn't had the energy to get to know any of them or wonder much about their stories, I found myself aching for the empty chairs.

I reached for her delicate, fine-boned hand and held it tight. Please, God, no empty chair here, I thought. She squeezed my hand in return.

The nurse finally came and got us. I held Mother's purse while she got on the scales. "You're up four pounds, Earline," the nurse said. "You must really be packing it away." Mother giggled like a schoolgirl and looked over at me and winked.

"I'm feeling so good," she told the nurse, sounding like the ladies on the commercials for vitamins or fiber supplements. "Tell her, Ann. Tell her how good I've been doing." She told them all about what she'd been eating. I didn't say anything. I just nodded and smiled, feeling as if we were seconds away from an execution. It didn't make sense to me to engage in peppy banter. I didn't talk because I couldn't. I was too afraid.

I hadn't been kidding myself. I was too fearful to let myself believe that the roller coaster was about to come to a complete stop. I was sure that it had just slowed down enough to fool me. With just one word from the doctor, it would speed up again and go careening right off the tracks.

When Dr. Leahy came in, I was seconds away from losing consciousness. I simply didn't know what to do.

She started right in, but I couldn't tell by the look on her face what she was going to say. No hint of a smile, no crinkle at the corners of the eyes. She went over to Mother and put her arm around her. I closed my eyes tight and started grinding my teeth, bracing myself for the next bad thing.

I could hear the papers rustling as Dr. Leahy flipped through the charts, but I was too busy mustering up the courage to go on to hear what she said.

"Did you hear that, Baby?" Mother said. She sounded happy, almost musical.

I remember opening only one eye, as if hearing really bad news with one eye open would make it only half as bad. "Sorry, I was distracted," I said and shook it off. Mother shot me one of those "Snap out of it, I need you to pay attention" looks.

"Your mother's white count is fabulous, and her CA125 blood test is normal, absolutely normal."

I looked at Dr. Leahy to make sure that I had heard her right. She was nodding and smiling. Then I looked at my mother, who had the biggest grin on her face.

"What does all of this mean?" I wanted to know.

"Well, we still need to schedule CAT scans, and then her second-look surgery to be sure. If all that comes out okay, it looks like the chemo worked," the doctor said. "We could be looking at a remission."

"We did it, we did it," Mother said. "I just knew it."

I don't know when it was that I lost my faith, or if I ever really had any. But never in my wildest dreams was I expecting anything other than to be dealt the final blow on that day in the doctor's office.

"Her blood work is normal?" I asked, to be sure that I wasn't simply wishing the words I wanted into her mouth.

"We do the other tests to confirm, but the preliminary blood work looks good," the doctor said. "Now we keep our fingers crossed."

I started to cry inconsolably. I'd gotten a gift that I hadn't dared wish for. I had some tangible hope. I couldn't have cried any harder if they had told me that my mother was going to die in two days. There were no words. This time Mother corralled me and our things out of the door. "Come on, Baby. Let's get you home."

Over the next few days, we celebrated. We shopped because she now felt like she was going to be around to wear nice clothes. We bought her silk pants and matching sweaters. We bought lipsticks and new foundation. "I want something that makes me look like I have some color. I've been so pale," she said.

She was making plans. "Life is too short, you have to be happy," she said. "I know I'm going to make myself happy."

I wondered what that meant.

We were all riding this wave of good news. Even the kids picked up on the vibe. The pall that had draped our house for months had suddenly lifted. Where we had made a point of trying to find something to laugh at every day, now the laughs were genuine and spontaneous, sometimes for no reason at all. Sometimes the tears were spontaneous too. I'd catch a glimpse of Nicole sitting on the floor getting her hair combed, and look into Mother's face, concentrating on every stroke of the brush, and it would overwhelm me. Sometimes when she was eating a meal, a whole meal, she would start to cry, remembering, I'm sure, what it was like when she couldn't eat, or couldn't keep anything down because of the chemo.

She started spending more time at her own apartment, cooking meals for John, who was around more. She was cleaning house, feeling normal. I was starting to feel normal too. I had forgotten what it was like to have a life that wasn't consumed by sickness and mortality. It seemed that the sun had come out for the first time since July.

It also got me thinking about what I wanted next. I had a job that I was glad to have, even though I knew that it wasn't giving me the challenges that I wanted. But it was perfect for a woman whose real job was being the primary caregiver for her mother. I started looking for some sign of what to do with myself now that it looked as if I didn't need to be a full-time caregiver anymore.

I thought about looking for a job that would give me more influence and more money. But I knew that there were things I didn't like about being a worker bee in some organization. I didn't love life at the water cooler. I didn't like office politics. I wasn't interested in hearing about dying cats or kids with the croup, all the gossip you are subjected to when you work with other people. I didn't want to move to someone else's vision of what my career should be and how fast it should progress. And most of all, I hated the idea that someone else controlled how much money I made.

I didn't know what I would do, but I knew that once I put my plan in action, I would never be in a situation where I had to ask anybody for a raise. It looked like I was headed toward being self-employed, but I didn't know how it was going to happen. Just thinking about it made me smile. Hoping for divine inspiration, every day I would quietly plan, and study, and read, in the same way I had become a student of cancer.

To my surprise and joy, Mother was planning her next steps too. She was thinking about a job, not for the money but for the normalcy. I went to her apartment for a visit and found her sitting at the kitchen table with a neat stack of job classifieds that she'd clipped out and a pad of paper. She was reworking her resume.

"I thought the whole point of retiring was to be retired," I said.

She looked up at me over the huge glasses that were once my grandmother's. "Retiring means doing what you want to do. I think after lying around, I *want* to work." She waited to see what I had to say.

"Well, if you want to do something, why don't you become a consultant? You could work out of your house and go see people when you need to," I said.

The idea of entrepreneurship didn't appeal to her at all. "I like having a job. That other stuff is too risky," she said. "Plus, I like being around people and getting dressed up every day."

One day she asked me to meet her for lunch and when we sat down, she slid an envelope across the table. "What's this?" I asked.

I opened it to find two plane tickets to Las Vegas.

"I want to go and I want you to go with me. Let's have some fun. We need some fun."

"But shouldn't you—"

"You never had a chance to come see me when we lived in Vegas." She had it all planned out. She had even found out that there was some show for Barbie collectors going on and set the date of the trip. That was the magic carrot.

After all we'd been through, how could I say no to anything she wanted? But I was slightly apprehensive. I'd never traveled with my mother as an adult. The last time we'd traveled together was in 1978, when we flew to Dallas to get me settled in my first job after college. She spent the trip telling me about the pitfalls of adult life. The world according to Mom. She did the talking, I did the nodding: "I understand, I understand." Then, like any prodigal daughter, I ignored everything she told me as soon as I put her back on the plane.

But I agreed to the Vegas trip. "Lucy and Ethel do Vegas, huh?"

It was a chance to celebrate how far we'd come. Everybody in the house was breathing a lot easier.

"Do you want me to go with you to the CAT scan and follow up?"

"No, I want to try to go by myself this time. I finally feel like I'm in control again," she said. "You go to work, and I'll call you when I'm done."

"But you've never been by yourself. I've always gone. Are you sure you want to do this alone?" I asked again. I was so proud of her, but there was a part of me that was worried. What if . . . ?

"No. I can do this one. Everything is okay. I just feel it. Everything will be normal," she said.

She was seeing her life round and full, and allowing her the freedom and control to go to Dr. Leahy by herself was all a part of being normal again.

TWENTY-ONE

The day Mother went back to see Dr. Leahy to get the results of the CAT scan, I went about my routine, going into the office, shuffling papers from one side of the desk to the other. The UPS man delivered a shipment of Barbies, which always broke up the morning. I made some calls and researched some grants. I couldn't stand being in my skin. I looked at my watch and it was only eleven o'clock. Mother's appointment was at twelve. I had to do something to keep myself busy, so I called my friend Brenda for one of our clandestine lunch meetings.

When I got back, I felt at peace somehow. Then the receptionist handed me a note. Call your mother ASAP.

I went in my office and closed the door, put my feet up on the desk, and hit the speed dial. I was thinking about what I could do for her to celebrate her good news.

"Hey, Ma. Tell me all about it," I said as soon as she picked up the phone, not giving her a chance to say hello. The pause on the other end was endless.

Finally she answered. It was that underwater voice again. "It's not good. It's not good."

I was out of the door and at her place in minutes. I don't even remember how I got there. I don't even remember running up the stairs to her apartment.

What I found when I got there was a beaten soul, a broken heart. I held her and let her cry in my arms. "I'm so sorry you went alone," I said. "I'm so mad at myself."

She tried to talk, saying a few words that I couldn't make out. Her body shook, it trembled. We must have sat like that for an hour as I rocked her as if she was the child and I was the mother. It took a lot of effort for me not to try to quiet her down. I owed it to her to let this shock run its course. My mind couldn't really imagine what the doctor had told her. How bad was bad? How awful was awful? How much time did we have left?

When she finally pulled back and smoothed out her clothes, I got up and got a cold washcloth for her face. "Tell me."

There wasn't much to tell. The CAT scan was dramatically different from the blood-work results. Basically, the tumor was growing and the cancer was spreading. The chemotherapy hadn't worked. She still had a cancer that could kill her.

"Why? Why is this happening?" she asked me.

I didn't have any answers. I was helpless. Everything was made worse by the fact that I had never seen her like this. I thought I had seen her hit bottom when Grandma died. That wasn't even close to this. I avoided saying the things people say. No words of encouragement. No words of defeat. I worked hard to get my face in a neutral position so that she couldn't read me. I pretended that I was with a stranger, that I was just a person who was there to listen, and maybe ask a few questions. To do anything else, to engage myself at this moment, would have been of no help to either of us, I thought. There needed to be someone who could think, who could plan.

The only question left to ask was "What do you want to do now?" She had to decide whether she was tired of fighting, or whether she wanted to try something else. The doctor, from what Mother explained, had not offered many other options. The best she could suggest was a stab at another, more powerful chemotherapy. But it might not work, and would definitely make her a whole lot sicker. "Whatever you want to do, I will support you. Just tell me what you want to do next."

To my surprise, she came out swinging. "I want to try something else."

So I came out swinging too. I immediately called Dr. Leahy and insisted that the oncologist get her into some kind of clinical trial. I demanded it.

"You have to understand, there aren't a lot of trials for cases this advanced. It's all experimental," Dr. Leahy said.

I wasn't having it. "Find one. Or I will."

"You know, even if she does get into a trial, there is no guarantee that she'll be one of the participants who gets the medicine. They're blind studies. Blind studies give a percentage of the participants the experimental drug, and another percentage of patients get placebos—pills that have no medicine in them."

"So what's the worst that could happen if she was one of the ones who got the placebo?" I wanted to know.

"The cancer would eat her up. It would run its natural course."

"And if she got the medicine?"

"You never know. But there are very few who have shown outstanding results with cases like your mother's. You might be setting her up for another big disappointment. They might not even accept her."

"Look, it seems that the studies and the doctors who are the gatekeepers to the studies don't make them available to minorities in the same way they are available to others." I had done my homework. African-American men and women were not included in clinical trials at the same rates as other patients. Most patients of color don't even know to ask about clinical trials. It is another way that the poor, the undeserved, and minorities are denied access to state-of-the-art care.

I knew that Dr. Leahy wasn't withholding care because of the color of Mother's skin or her ability to pay. The insurance was good. In my heart, I knew that everything she was saying about the trials was true. But I also knew that I would try anything and everything I knew to get Mother just one more shot. If I had to make loud, threatening noises, I would. Nothing personal.

Two days later, the doctor's office called with information about a clinical trial at the National Institutes of Health in Bethesda, Maryland. Mother had to go there and go through some preliminary testing to see if she met the study's criteria.

TWENTY-TWO

A few days later, Mother headed off to Bethesda on her own. "I need to start doing this stuff for myself," she said. "When I get accepted, and have to go back, then I want you to go with me. Let me do this one."

She did. I took her to the airport at five-thirty in the morning. John picked her up at seven-thirty that night.

When I talked to her that night, she said very little. "They poked and punched and had me pee in cups all day." She was also fascinated by the people in the waiting room. The cancer patients shared a waiting room with persons living with AIDS, who were either being tested to get into a clinical trial, or were on some new protocol and were being monitored. "Some of them were sicker than me," she said. "But everybody was very nice."

She was hopeful but unusually aware of the possibility that she might not be accepted. I wrote it off to her having had such a long day and being tired. She was more interested in talking about the people with AIDS. "Do you think they have it worse?" she asked.

"Who?"

"Those poor people with AIDS. Do they have it worse than me? There was a woman there who had little kids. She was so sick." She had spent so much of the day waiting that she'd heard how hard it was for other patients who had been abandoned by their friends and families. She'd gotten to know what it was like to lose your job and your coverage. "It's just an awful, sad thing," she said.

Later in the conversation she said, "Find an AIDS organization here. One that helps people buy medicine and get food. I want to send them some money."

The next afternoon the call came. Mother had not made it into the study. The tests found that she had impaired kidney function. She would have to get that treated first, then in a few months she could apply again. I didn't know if she even had a few months left.

She was absolutely serene in accepting the news. It was as if she knew.

"Did they tell you this in Bethesda?" I asked. "You knew this yesterday?"

She didn't answer me directly. But it was obvious that she had come back with more information than she had initially shared with me. "I want to go on that trip to Las Vegas before they do any surgery to find out what's wrong with my kidneys, okay?"

TWENTY-THREE

Even though I initially said no, I didn't have the heart to put my foot down. There were a million reasons not to take on such a trip. What if she was getting worse and was really too fragile to travel? What if, God forbid, she died on me right in Las Vegas?

But she begged and cajoled me. "I promise, I feel good. I really do."

My resistance was melting because I wasn't sure that it wouldn't be her last trip and I didn't have the heart to deny her something she seemed to need so badly. I got the doctor to confirm that she could survive it, then I made her promise me that if she got sick while we were gone—the least bit sick—she would come back with me immediately with no arguments. The following week we landed in Las Vegas.

Her transformation was amazing. As soon as we got off the plane, her face lit up, her steps got quicker, and whatever disappointment Bethesda had given her was waved away by the magic wand of the Strip. Mother knew her way around the

Strip the way I knew my way around those over-size, twenty-four-hour supermarkets that sell boats and refrigerators and bulbs of elephant garlic. She was in her element.

After a good night's sleep, we started our first day in Vegas at her favorite breakfast place in one of the casinos. Why a woman who could only take in thimblefuls of food at any one meal would want to stand in a line that snaked back and forth like so many feet of gnarled intestine just to eat breakfast was beyond me. The hundreds of people waiting for bacon and eggs reminded me of the old Depression-era newsreels of people standing in bread lines to get their families through the week. The only thing missing was background music . . . Barbra Streisand singing "Brother, Can You Spare a Dime?" Instead we inched toward the spiral-carved ham to the mystical tones of Wayne Newton's "Danke Schoen."

"Wait till you see everything that's in there," she said, her face glowing with the joy I had seen on it when she'd introduced me to Santa Claus, maple-cluster candies, and designer discount shopping. Today she was introducing me to the sensuous culinary pleasures of the biggest slough and trough known to man, woman, or leisure-suit-wearing-beast.

I was totally grossed out. Old people were picking their noses in this line. Men had hair so long growing out of their ears that you could have cornrowed it with little effort. It was official: I had entered dining hell.

It didn't take long to figure out why they called this casino Circus Circus. Once we paid, I was shocked and amazed to find the biggest spread I have ever seen . . . of dorm food. There were tons of greasy bacon, timeworn pancakes, and something that looked like the powdered eggs they'd served us at Indiana University. I couldn't believe that we waited a half hour in line for dorm food. "Isn't it something?" Mother said.

"Yes," I agreed. "It really is *something.*"

She was having a ball, piling her plate with bacon, waffles, potatoes, you name it. But when we got to the table, she'd take a bite of sausage, then a waitress would clear away her plate and she would get up and get another one. It was the idea of being engaged in the food more than the food itself that was making her happy. She even started in on my plate, stabbing a piece of ham, then tearing off the tiniest bit and eating it. "Isn't it good?"

"Ummm, really good," I agreed. The omelet wasn't bad. But I wasn't touching the grits, no matter how much shredded cheese was in them. "Delicious," I said, throwing out my childhood code word.

I was being sufficiently gracious, or so I thought. Then the pressures of having to be so good got to me. I saw the soft-serve machines and I gave in to temptation. "I'll be right back," I said.

I looked around in case there was some high roller from Gary who might recognize me. Then I checked to make sure Mother was occupied with the plate I had just heaped with mashed potatoes and fried fish. The coast was clear.

I stuck my head under the spout of the chocolate-French-vanilla swirl and went for it. Who hasn't wanted to do that? I was learning that moments of bliss like this were not guaranteed. So if you are waiting for just the right time to stick your head under the spout of a soft-serve machine, it will never quite present itself. You gotta just boldly stick your little face right in there. It helped that I wasn't ever going to see these people again.

It was the most amazing experience. Like running through the lawn sprinkler with your church clothes on. I ummmed and ahhhhed. It was good. Good-sex good. Fabulous-shoe good. So good that it made me laugh until soft serve came spraying out of my nose.

"What are you doing?"

I turned around, with soft serve oozing out of the sides of

my mouth, to see my mother with her tiny hands on her tiny hips. I said what I thought was "Nothing, Ma." But my denial was refuted by the evidence. She cuffed me on the back of the head with her hand.

It was worth it.

After being sufficiently chastised, I headed off with her to the casino. Even when it's eleven in the morning, inside a casino it feels like night. With the flashing lights of the machines and the neon signs, I never knew what time it was.

As surprised as I was by Mother's stamina at the slots, she couldn't hold a candle to the people who were playing three or four machines at a time, lining up their big cardboard buckets for a catch. Mother was content to play her slots one at a time, moving to another machine when she thought she had milked the first one dry.

After a while, she'd say "please" and "thank you," to it, tell it that it was stupid, dried up, cold, or whatever slot machine crack heads say when they have caught the flashing-light fever. I would have been concerned, but for the first time in months, she didn't look the least bit sick or even worried about being sick. It could have been the lighting, but I think that just as I was losing track of time, she was losing her cancer and her worries in a way that chemo and the meditative visualization of her little costume jewelry butterflies hadn't been able to do. Even when she was losing, she was grinning. She'd feel my eyes studying her and look up over her glasses for just a hot second, wink, and go back to work with her one-armed bandit.

I got the feeling that she could stay in that same spot forever. People were nice. Waitresses brought her cocktails for a quarter. Hungry? They brought these funky little shrimp cocktails, so you never had to get up. Sitting in this place where the hours folded into each other, she looked as if she knew time couldn't run out on her here.

Once, a few months before the Vegas trip, she and I were stringing beans for dinner, talking about nothing in particular. She came clean.

"I knew something was wrong. I was just too afraid to go to the doctor." It was the first time she had admitted that she knew she really needed medical attention but had ignored her instincts.

"I knew it was bad. So I went to the casino every day," she said. "Like I used to go shopping."

"How can you afford to do that every day?"

"I'd lose some. I'd win some," she said. "I usually broke even."

I couldn't imagine losing money like that. "Is it that much fun?"

She got this gauzy, faraway smile on her face, looked at me with tears in her eyes, and said, "I could forget."

At that moment it dawned on me. "Where were you that day in July? The day you—"

"Had to go to the hospital?" she finished my sentence. I nodded.

She concentrated on snapping the beans and said, "At the casino."

I thought about that conversation as she perched on her gambling stool, grinning every time a blue or a green or a red light flashed in her face, and understood.

So here we were. "Why don't you play? You can't come to Las Vegas and just watch," she said.

I was content just to watch. My philosophy on gambling is simple. It's like taking a twenty-dollar bill and striking a match to it. "The idea of spending two hundred dollars and not coming back with a pair of shoes or a bag of books to show for it is too deep for me," I said.

"You are so old sometimes," she said. "It's Las Vegas." She

poured out half a cup of quarters into another paper bucket and handed it to me. "Go play."

Off I went. I put in a quarter, pulled the slot machine arm or pushed the button—which took a lot less energy—and watched two lemons and a cherry, or a cherry, a grape, and an apple come up. I lost again and again. Then I got braver and put two or three quarters in at a time, which meant that at least I would get done faster. I was so bored by the process of losing that when I heard the machine chime and play music and heard the coins hit the bucket like a hailstorm, I assumed the person to the left or to the right of me had won. The woman who was sitting on the stool next to me pointed to my machine, which spit quarters for what seemed to be about fifteen minutes. I was so excited I screamed, "Oh, shit, oh, shit."

I jumped up to tell my mother, but the lady caught me by my shirttail. "Hon, you can't go running off without your winnings. They won't be here when you get back."

So I took my bucketful of loot, picked up my purse, found Mother, and announced that I was ready to go. She flagged down one of the women in the short skirts and the tight white shirts who worked for the casino to cash in my winnings for me. She came back and counted out a cool, crisp $300. I offered Mother half of the winnings, but she declined.

"Why don't you go down to the Fashion Center? There's a Neiman's there. Do a little shopping. Buy the kids something. Go to Caesar's. There are some shops there."

I was being sent off to play by a woman who had cuffed me on the back of the head that very morning for living out my fantasies with an ice-cream machine. We agreed to meet at the hotel in a few hours. I left her the rental car and happily headed out on foot, still hearing the music of the coins hitting the bucket.

Outside, I was blinded by broad daylight. It became clear

that the shops at Caesar's Palace were the place to be if you were a guy who wore thick gold serpentine chains with gold medallions the size of cabbages, a Las Vegas showgirl, or if you were a boy named Bambi. As a people watcher, I was in heaven.

I finally hit a shoe store, a really good shoe store. Hold me back. I wear a size six, which is usually the display size, but every shoe I picked up was a twelve or larger. Any self-respecting shoe goddess knows that retailers always put out the smallest size as the display. I'd never even seen shoes this big. Before I knew it, I thought out loud, "What the hell is this, a shoe store for transvestites?"

And then this beautiful saleswoman with flawless makeup, who sounded like the Voice of CNN, tapped me on the shoulder. "Why yes, honey, it is."

I looked up at her, then around at the other customers and realized that I was the only woman in the joint with my own female parts. They gathered around me to study my tiny feet. "Doll Feet," they called me. I sat and watched them try on shoes, and gave my opinion on color and the way the heel of the shoe lifts the calf. In return, they gave me advice on how to wax my brows for more drama and schooled me on filling in my lips with lip pencil before putting on my lipstick.

I was a little giddy with all the girl talk. It didn't matter to me that the girls were really guys.

After working my way through Caesar's, then Neiman's, then Saks, I met Mother at the hotel room and took a nap before heading out again. That night we moved on to another casino, where we muscled our way up to the crap tables like old pros.

She had a knack for making friends wherever she went, and the dice table was no exception. "I'm Earline, and I used to live here, but now I live in Lansing with my Baby, here," she said to a woman in a red dress that plunged to her navel, exposing breasts that sat on her chest like big bowling balls. I couldn't tell you what her face looked like or if she even had a face.

Then Mother introduced me to the man next to her. "Say hello to Joe, Baby." Joe smiled at me with the one tooth left in his head, which was gold. "Pleased to meet you, Baby." He winked at me.

I had this horrible flash of my mother being swept up in a torrid weekend fling with one-toothed Joe. What if he ended up being my next stepfather? What if . . . ? I made a mental note to myself to be nicer to John when I got back.

Just when I was sure that this couldn't get any worse, Mother insisted that I blow on the dice that she cupped in her hands. I knew that she wouldn't leave me alone until I did, so I reluctantly complied, pretending that I was blowing out the birthday candles, wishing that we could just go back to the room. "Just stop calling me Baby, okay?"

"Baby needs a new pair of shoes," she shouted and threw them. People craned their necks to see what kind of shoes Baby was wearing, if she really needed new ones. The dice rolled and bounced until they found their spot. *Two sixes, a winner.* Then she hit another winner, and another. She decided to pull back most of the money and leave only a fraction of each win on the table. It was a good strategy because after a few lucky turns, she started to lose. Snake eyes, craps, cold dice, bad news. Her breathing got more labored, so we called it a night.

As we walked back to the elevators, arm in arm to support her steps, I had a minor stroke of genius that I knew would forever put an end to that Baby stuff.

"Please stop calling me Baby in public, especially here."

She stopped walking. "Why does it make a difference here? We don't know them."

"Well," I whispered, looking around as if I cared that these strangers might hear us, pausing and breathing deeply for effect, "they might think we are *lipstick lesbians.*" I had just learned this term in the shoe store. I knew that it would come in handy eventually, I just didn't think it would be so soon.

Her already large eyes grew to twice their normal size. "What on earth is that?"

I had learned that lesbians came in all shapes and sizes and were just as interesting and universal as everyone else. However, Mother's world was not nearly as global. She knew a few in her day and always thought that they could be identified by their own brand of scarlet letter. In her world, they were tagged by mustaches and five o'clock shadow. She thought they all had marine-issue buzz cuts slicked back by Brylcreem. According to Mother, they wore chinos and men's white undershirts and packs of cigarettes in their sleeves, whether they smoked or not.

"They're lesbians who don't look like lesbians," I said matter-of-factly.

"Why would anybody think we were like that?"

"Well, we are two grown women, but we don't wear signs that tell the world that say we are mother and daughter. And with you calling me *Baby* all the time . . ." I shrugged again.

She was squinting at me to see if I was putting her on when I hit her with another punch. "They say Greta Garbo slept with women."

"She was a . . . what did you call it? Lipstick thing?"

I just shrugged again. "There are lesbians who look just like us, girly girls." This upset everything she knew about the world. She found a stool by the elevator and sat fanning herself, studying every woman who passed by us.

"I don't believe it. That's crazy," she said. "You're just saying that because you hate it when I call you that." True.

It was time to take her down for the Las Vegas count. I outed someone that I knew from childhood who my mother had always held up as the perfect specimen of female pulchritude. "Carol is gay." I said. Carol was not gay at all, but she was sufficiently beautiful and feminine for Mother to get the point. Plus, she was evil and bitchy and dumb as a post, and called me Gap all through high school because my teeth were three carlengths apart. My mothers' mouth was wide open and stayed that way for a long time.

"Close your mouth, Mama. Carol's not gay."

"Okay, Bab—okay, Ann."

Day three of our trip was the day of the big Barbie show—three hundred collectors and dealers in one room. I was going to attend workshops on green-eared Barbies, Barbie's relationship to Ken and Skipper, the difference between mint and nearly mint outfits worn by Barbie and her friends. Mother planned to spend the day with one of her friends from Gary who had moved to Vegas.

I called the hotel room several times, but didn't reach her. I was happy to imagine her doing some wicked gossiping and shopping with her friend, having a good time with someone other than me. She was out somewhere being normal.

When I got back to the room at about five o'clock, loaded down with shopping bags chock full of dolls and clothes and books about dolls and clothes, she was in her nightgown, staring out the window.

"How was lunch with Mae?" I asked.

"Fine." The answer was clipped and strained. She never turned around to look at me.

"Did you get back and put your nightgown on?"

She didn't answer, but I could see that she was holding a balled-up tissue in her hand. The energy in the room was all wrong.

"Look at me," I said. "What's up?" I was scared. When she turned around, I could see that her eyes were red and swollen from crying. "Did you get stood up?"

"No," she said. "I didn't call." She told me that she was tired and had started hurting. She'd been in that room all day.

I felt terrible and terrified. "I called to check on you, why didn't you answer?" I dropped my loot on the bed and walked over to her. "I'd have come right back."

"I know. I didn't want to ruin your day. You deserved it."

"So you sat in this room, sick and alone?"

She nodded.

I thought for a minute. "We're leaving. I'll get us packed." I was feeling in my bones that something awful was about to happen. What would I do if she was taking a terrible turn and I couldn't get her back home?

"No. Please, let's stay. I just probably pushed myself too hard yesterday." She took a sip of water. "I feel better now." But she didn't look better. She looked like she had shrunk since the morning. She was pale. Her hands trembled when she wiped her eyes.

"We had a deal." I was the firm disciplinarian now. In my best Ward Cleaver voice, I reasoned with her. "We have to go back now. I don't know what's wrong. There is something wrong. You are a million miles away from your doctor." I fished around in my purse for the tickets so I could call the airline. "I can't take care of you here."

She was crying hard then. She buried her face in her hands. I could hardly hear her. "I just want to be okay again. What if they're right? What if the books and the doctors and the tests are really right? Ann, what if I'm not going to get well?"

Okay, Miss Smarty Pants, who has all the answers to every damn thing that passes your way, what was the answer to that question?

The only thing I could do was pray all night that she wasn't slipping away, then get her home as fast as I could in the morning. I stayed up to listen to her breathe, and I kept waking her up to make sure she wasn't dead. "Ma, you doing okay?"

Andrea King Collier

If we'd come into town on our own steam, we left much differently. I used a wheelchair to get her to the hotel lobby. At the airport, we got a ride on one of those little cars that beeps as it travels to the boarding gates. Once we got on the plane in one piece, I did something I never did. I ordered one of those drinks in those tiny bottles. She cried all the way home. The roller coaster was speeding up, but we couldn't get off.

TWENTY-FOUR

As soon as we got back home, I called the doctor's emergency number and reported what had happened on the trip. Mother was admitted to the hospital first thing on Monday and had emergency surgery that afternoon to make sure that her new symptoms weren't caused by the kidney problems that the NIH had detected. Dr. Leahy promised us that they would try to fix whatever it was so that the clinical trial might reconsider her.

The tests showed that Mother's kidneys were indeed failing. The surgeon was going to try to put a tiny shunt in to get full function back. We were back to more waiting, more praying. It was like reliving that first surgery all over again, only this time with the knowledge of everything that could go wrong. Every time we came back here, my biggest wish was just to be able to see her and talk to her again. I did myself a favor and refused to think much about what might lie ahead.

After the surgery was completed, Dr. Leahy walked into the waiting room and motioned for me to come into the hall.

I was talking fast about nothing and everything. "I found another trial that will take her, once the kidney is functioning, and—"

"The tumor mass is too big," Dr. Leahy said, silencing any hopes I had for a miracle cure.

"We could give her more chemotherapy to try to shrink it down some. But, I have to be honest and tell you that it's only buying a little time."

"What are you telling me?"

"I guess I'm telling you that it's time to start thinking about hospice," she said.

There it was, out in the open. Hospice looms as huge as cancer. Cancer is a big, bad, scary word that hovers over a family like a cloud that will never go away. But after you've said it and explained it so many times, the "C" word begins to lose its shock value. If you've lived with it for a year or more, hearing "cancer" doesn't make the hair stand up on the back of your neck. It slowly becomes that unwanted relative who stays way too long, eats all your ice cream, puts his feet up on your cocktail table, and runs up your long-distance phone bill. I'd just gotten used to cancer. Now there was a storm brewing—Hurricane Hospice, threatening to blow my house down. And it scared me.

"It doesn't mean that you are going to lose her any day now," Dr. Leahy said, leaning in to make sure that I was paying attention to her. "It just means that it's time to get ready. Some people last in hospice care for six months, even longer."

I didn't care about some people. Some people go into remission. Some people get snatched from death's door. I just cared about my mother waiting for me to come back and tell her when she could get into another clinical trial.

"What are you saying, then? This is it?" I felt myself getting loud. "Six more months? That's all?"

Dr. Leahy looked at the door, cautioning me to lower my voice so my mother wouldn't hear me. "I don't think so. I don't know."

Every single day for one year I'd been a cheerleader telling her she had to believe that she would get well. She had to believe it like she'd never believed in anything else before. If she didn't believe that she would be cured, she wouldn't. All the literature said it. But if I threw in the towel and let them call in hospice, then she'd know that it was all over. She wouldn't fight.

"Hospice. That's what you want me to tell her?" I looked into the doctor's eyes for anything resembling a scrap of hope. "You want me to march my ass in there and tell her that there has been a little change of plan? 'Sorry, Mom, we're not doing clinical trials. We're not looking for the magic bullet. Oops, I lied. You never stood a chance. Change of plan. We're doing hospice now.' That's what I say?"

"No. That's what I want the two of you to think about. I'll tell her, if you want."

"No. If it gets told, I tell her." I didn't know much, but I knew that when the time came, it had to come from me.

"Somehow I knew that," she said and nodded.

She put her hand lightly on my shoulder. "Hospice isn't a bad thing. It's a wonderful support system. You're going to need some help. More help than you can muster. This is where it gets rough."

I laughed. "You mean the last year wasn't rough? It was just a dress rehearsal for rough?"

She hugged me, and held me tight so I could get a good cry out before I went back in. She smelled like rosewater and rubbing alcohol. I felt the crush of her stethoscope against my chest and pulled back.

"I can't break down now. There's too much that still has to

be done. I don't know that we aren't still fighting. I don't see any towel to throw in yet."

"You've got to let yourself feel it eventually, Andrea. If you don't come to grips with it, she won't be able to either."

I shook off the tears. "Let's go in there and give her something. Not hospice, I have to think about that. But something." I needed to stall until I figured out what to do. There was nobody to help me get through this one. None of the books that I'd read over those months prepared me for this moment. If it did, I'd skimmed over it, looking for more optimistic sections. I felt the whole weight of this fight riding on my shoulders, pulling me down.

We found her sitting up in the bed telling jokes to the nurse, the two of them giggling like teenagers. "Hey, Baby," she said, then instantly corrected herself. "Ann."

"Hey, Mom." I didn't know what to do with my eyes. If I got too close to her, she would see the panic and the defeat in them. If I didn't look at her, she'd know it was bad news. So I took my chances with looking at her, but she always knew when I was lying.

"I've got one of my headaches." I rubbed my temples. "Just too tired, I guess."

I kissed her on the forehead and told her I needed to get some rest, then left. I was determined not to have a meltdown until I got home. I refused to think about it. I turned on the tape in the car and lost myself in the music. It was Billie Holiday.

When I got home, I walked right past Darnay and the kids, who were having a very noisy, burned, mystery meal. I climbed up the stairs, literally pulling myself up by the railing. When I finally got to my room, I shut the door, crawled to the bed with all my clothes on, still clutching my purse, because it was the only thing I had to hold on to, and wept.

I cried for the days when she hadn't wanted to participate in this ugly treatment and I'd made her. I cried for all the times that I'd sworn to her that it was going to be all right. I'd promised. I cried for that day when she'd found out that the treatments hadn't worked. I cried for all the research and all the phone calls. On some level, I'd never cared what the research had said because it had been grim from the beginning. But I had been determined to pull my mother through out of sheer will.

I fought and I fought and I prayed, then I fought some more. My mother and grandparents raised me to believe that with God's help, anything was possible. All I had to do was roll up my sleeves to make it happen. Hadn't I wanted it badly enough? Was some deep-seated resentment keeping me from making her well? How could I have failed her on something as important as this? I cried because this was the first time in this whole horrible adventure that I ever thought I couldn't fix it.

I cried because I finally got it. This was about something other than me and my ability to knit together the strength to pull us through. It was about more than my skill at researching and networking and tapping into resources. It was about Mother, and God's time, and fate, and the inevitable. I couldn't fix any of it, and until that moment I didn't really understand that the power wasn't mine. I fell asleep from despair and exhaustion and slept for a whole day.

෨

A few days later, Mother came to my house to recuperate from the surgery before heading back to her apartment. Short of telling Darnay, I hadn't said a word to Mother or John about what Dr. Leahy had told me. I didn't have to. Mother was happily taking chemo in pill form twice a day.

This was my first experience of my mother taking the pills. The two-day privacy rule that she had set down during the first round of treatment didn't apply at my house. I had handled most things well, but this particular chemo caused violent vomiting exactly one hour after she took the pill. It would have been easier to watch if I hadn't been carrying around the little secret that she was going through all of this for nothing. Who knew? Maybe it would help somehow. Maybe God would give us a reprieve.

After every vomiting session, I'd clean her up. We'd change her pajamas and the sheets, if needed. She'd settle in for a well-earned nap and I'd ask the same question as I tucked her in, "Do you still want to keep doing this? You don't have to keep doing this."

She always said the same thing. "It's not so bad. Not nearly as bad as before." So it went on that way for several days. What little I could get her to eat she wasn't able to keep down, so it seemed that she got smaller every day. I went back to eating for two.

The doctor ordered home health nurses to draw blood and check vitals. Mother never had a chance to hate the nurses, as she was wont to do, because there was a different nurse every day. Each brought a flying blur of activity and orders. *Arm please. Vein please. Did you vomit today? Did you pee today? 'Bye.*

On the fifth day, the phone rang. It was Dr. Leahy. She'd gotten some additional lab reports. Mother's white-cell count numbers were going through the roof and the results of the CA125 tests were "off the charts," all signs that her cancer was raging out of control. "The treatments aren't working. They're just making her sick and uncomfortable for no reason. She's going to start having some pretty rough pain," the doctor said, and then there was an endless pause. "Her MRI showed the beginning of some brain involvement. It's time."

TWENTY-FIVE

John and I had been pretty successful in avoiding each other, but now I called him and asked him to come over. When he pulled up, I was sitting on the front porch waiting to head him off at the pass. I asked him to go for a walk with me and told him what I knew and that she had to be told. I also told him about hospice.

"No," he said. "It's not right." He stopped and folded his arms, as if he had spoken the last word on the subject. Then we started walking again, and I picked up the pace.

"What the hell am I supposed to do, let her think she's going to be okay? Is she supposed to wake up and find out that she's dead? What the hell is that?" Then I noticed that he was about half a block behind me. He caught up and we kept going.

"I say no. I vote no," he said.

"What exactly is it that you think you are voting on?" That she wouldn't die? Was this a "no-hospice" vote? Was this the vote not to tell her that we'd run out of medical options? I think I tried to be kind, or as kind as I could be under the circumstances, but soon enough my patience ran out. I had no time or energy to provide compassionate care for anybody but my mother.

"I'm sorry. You have no vote here. I'm telling you because you have a right to know," I said. "It's been me here. I've been the one on the firing line. You've been the one making cameo appearances. I stopped judging it a long time ago. But if you think you are going to come in and decide anything other than to continue to cooperate, you are wrong."

"How are you going to tell me that I don't have a vote?" He was angry and, looking back on it, I don't blame him, but I didn't give an inch. We were squarely and resolutely in each other's faces.

"You lost your vote when you left me here to deal with all this by myself. You lost your vote when you went off to play Viva Las Vegas or whatever you were doing." My head started throbbing. I was having a hard time catching my breath. I knew that we were going to have a big knock-down, drag-out fight, but I wasn't anticipating doing it in front of my neighbors as they planted pink geraniums in hanging baskets. Dogs barked at us. Kids on bikes shook their heads in disgust. *Silly, crazy adults.*

"I just don't think it's right, that's all. It's like playing God," he said. Tears rolled down his face, and he wiped them away with the back of his hand. I got a glimpse of his wedding band as the sun hit it. He was right, it was like playing God. I knew what was going to happen once I told her. I was reminded as I looked at him that he was her husband, no matter what I thought of the role he played in taking care of her. He did have a vote.

"I just don't know what else to do," I said. "She's going to wonder what's next, John. The problem is that there is no next. This is as good as it gets." I had made a lifelong commitment to never let him see me cry and this didn't seem like the best time to break that policy. But I felt tears rolling down my own face. I tried to hold them back the way that children do, telling myself that I wasn't going to cry. I held out my hand to him and we walked arm in arm up the long driveway. When we got to the house, he turned to me and said, "I still vote no." The truce melted in the early June sunlight and lay in a pool at our feet.

"You still talking about a vote?" I asked in disbelief. "Let me tell you what your vote means," I said, jabbing my finger into his chest. "It means that you take her home right now and do hospice there. It means that you'll be the one feeding her through a tube, if and when it comes to that. It means that it all falls on you." I was sputtering and flailing my arms. "Vote that it all falls on you. Vote for that, damnit."

"Okay, okay."

"Okay?" I asked, waiting for clarification.

"Okay, handle it your way. You win."

I softened again, because I wanted him to understand that I didn't have the answers either. I was just doing the best I knew how with what we'd been given. He needed to understand that I would have done anything not to have to be in that awful spot.

"John, if I had my way, she would be well. If I had my way, I'd have my mother for a long, long time." I shook my head. "No, it's not anywhere close to being my way. If I won, then she would be here to see my kids grow up. But she won't. Nobody wins here. Nobody wins."

We sat on the porch together in silence, contemplating what lay ahead. Then he took the kids out for ice cream so that I could talk to her uninterrupted. I fixed myself a rum and Coke, more rum than Coke, a little courage in a bottle, gulped it down, then headed upstairs.

TWENTY-SIX

"Mom, something has come up," I said, crawling in the bed next to her. "Things are happening faster than Dr. Leahy thought, and she doesn't know how to fix them. I don't know how to fix them either, Mommy." They were such hard words to say. "If you still want to fight this thing, I will fight with you. I'll do whatever you want me to do."

"What's next, then?" she asked. Because I was holding her, I couldn't see her face but I could feel the tears, and I could hear the soft quiver in her voice.

I just shrugged. I had told little lies to keep her going before, but not today. "I don't know."

"So what do we do?"

I suggested that we start the hospice process.

"That woman, Cinnamon, is not coming back, is she?"

"No, Mom. *Ginger* isn't coming back. But Dr. Leahy thinks we need some different help now. I can't keep you comfortable by myself anymore." I squeezed her tight to me.

"Yesterday you did," she said. "What's different about today?" She sounded like a small child who didn't understand what had changed.

Again, I looked away, hoping what I didn't say would be enough. And it was.

"We fought so hard, didn't we?"

"Yes, we did," I said. "We absolutely did. And we still can. Only you can say when we stop."

TWENTY-SEVEN

Later that evening, after Darnay had tucked Nicole and Christopher in for the night, Mother asked me to tell her the Uncle Marcel story again. It was almost impossible to tell. Each word burned my throat as it came out. After I was done, she said, "There won't be a visitor with a suitcase, will there?" It was the last time she asked for that story.

The next day when I went in to check on her, she handed me a list, carefully written in a spiral-bound notebook, her own little Command Central. "I need you to make the calls now."

I called each person on the list, explaining, apologizing for keeping the secret for so long. I didn't let any call last longer than ten minutes, then I was on to the next one. Many of them asked to speak to her. Some calls she took and others she waved off. I told them that she was asleep. She insisted that I tell all the female relatives on the list to make sure to get their annual exams. "Breast and ovarian cancers might have some genetic link, so we all have to stay on top of it. Okay?"

It was awful to relay this information over and over again. A month before, I had thought we were out of the woods, and now I had to tell everyone who was close to us that my mother had cancer and that she was going to die. I put the hardest one off until last, not really sure that I could make it. I was hoping that breaking the news so many times would make it easier. It didn't.

"Grandpa, it's Ann," I said. "I have something to tell you."

He waited. When a person has lived to be eighty-six years old, he has gotten many calls that started that way, and they were never good news. I could almost see him feel his way along the edge of the table, and make his way to the sink. He put his hand over the phone and said, "Ruby, put some ice in a glass for me, will you?"

I heard him shut off the water and take a sip. I heard the ice clinking around. I could close my eyes and see his Adam's apple bob. I could see him sit down in his chair at the kitchen table. "Turn the television down so I can hear," he said.

"I've been keeping something from you. That's the truth."

"Yeah?"

"Yeah. Now I have to tell you what's going on. Mama's been really sick since she came here to live. She has cancer." I reached out and held my mother's hand. Up to now, to get through telling everyone else, I had been able to put my heart on automatic pilot. This time it was like digging out pieces of my heart and throwing them across the room. The insides of my throat hurt.

"Oh," he said.

"She has ovarian cancer, and she's been here getting treatment. I didn't tell you because she didn't want anybody to know, at least not until she got well."

"Well," he repeated.

"It seems that she's not going to get well." I felt Mother

squeeze my hand to help me get through it. "We're doing hospice care, like they did with Brother. But we're doing it here, in our house."

He wanted to know if I had told the others. His other children. His surviving family. I had. There was something in his throat too. It was low and deep, maybe a cry, then it was gone. His few remaining words to me came out like little trembles. "Here we go again."

This was the first time that I thought I wouldn't live through this. It was easier when nobody knew, although it had been a hard, terrible secret to keep. At least when we were the only ones who knew, I didn't have to worry about anybody else's pain.

"Would you like to speak to her? She's here. She's sitting here with me." I waited for the cue from him.

There was another long pause. His hand was over the phone again, so I couldn't hear what was going on. "Ann, let me call you right back. Tell her I need to call her right back." He tried to hang up and must have dropped the phone. I could hear him cry as he finally clicked off.

"What happened?" she asked me as I hung up. "What did he say?"

"He said he'd call you back." I shrugged.

About a half hour later he did call back and Mother answered the phone. She nodded, as if he could see her. She cried. Finally, she said, "Okay, Daddy. I love you too." Then she handed the phone to me.

He made small talk. He never said the word "cancer." He cried, then he pulled himself together and made more small talk. It took him a while to work his way into something resembling a real conversation about what was going on with Mother.

"So, how are you doing?" he asked.

"Okay. It's been tough."

I told him that the others were probably going to drive up to see Mother that weekend. He could ride with them.

"I can't. I told her I couldn't. Can't bear it." He was crying again. "Let me tell you something. It doesn't help me much now, but it might help you sometime during this."

I waited. Anything that would help me get through this was worth waiting for. When I was a kid, he was my rock. He always knew what to say to make me feel better, more whole. From scraped knees to not getting jobs I wanted, he was the man I always wanted on my side. It was his voice I always wanted to hear.

"One of two things happens in this world. Either you out-live your parent, or your parent outlives you. Either you outlive your child, or your child outlives you. You get me?"

No, I didn't.

"I'm an old man. I've seen a lot. I've lost a lot," he said. "The worst was when I lost Lucille. It still is."

"I know, Grandpa."

"I have outlived a parent, two. And that is the natural order of the world. It's the way things are supposed to happen. It's what's happening to you, now. I also outlived a child."

He was talking about my aunt Gladys, who died of tuber-culosis when she was just fourteen years old. It was the crack in his armor. She'd been dead for over fifty years, and when he talked of it, which wasn't often, he spoke as if it had happened only last month.

"I never thought I'd outlive two of my kids. Earline would never have been able to stand outliving you. You know that's true. It is as it has to be."

"You did it somehow," I said. I was crying now.

"No. I did what I had to. I had a wife. I had three other little kids. Little children. It was the Depression. I had to get up. But I was lost. You should never have to live to see your child waste away and die." He broke down, which was unbearable for me. Nothing that could happen would be worse than this moment, I thought.

"Now I have to live to see another child of mine leave here. That is unnatural. She was supposed to see me go. That was what was natural. What you've been doing is hard. What you still have to do is hard. Almost too hard for a little girl like you, I know." He was calmer and stronger than I had heard him be since my grandmother died.

"When it gets tough, so tough you can't do any more, then go look at your kids. Losing your child is the worst," he said and hung up.

I couldn't get what my grandfather said out of my mind. I'd never considered that there would be a pain greater than losing my mother. "What would it be like for you now, if it was me?" I asked her. "If you were in my spot?"

She got a fierce, twisted look on her face. "Why would you ask such a thing? Why would you even bring such a thing up?" It was a curse that should never be said aloud or it might come true. She knew the law of nature too.

"He said it. I hadn't thought about it in that way," I said. It made me nervous. There was something so frightening about it. The death of a mother. The possibility of the death of a child. "He said he knew what it was like on both sides."

"Gladys," she said, sounding weary. "He adored her. Mother did too, but she held it inside," she said, referring to my grandmother.

Aunt Gladys was named after her. After Gladys died, my grandmother couldn't even say the name. She took her middle name, Lucille, as her first name after that. I hadn't thought about it much, but as my mother talked about those days, when Gladys was so sick, and when she went to the TB sanitarium, and what it was like for the younger kids, it occurred to me that

I had never heard my grandmother speak of it. It hurt my grandma so badly to say her own name, her given name, because it reminded her of the child she couldn't save. She just stopped saying it.

All that I knew about Aunt Gladys had come from him. The only picture of her that existed sat on his bedroom dresser.

"He was different after she died. His heart broke, I think," she said. "My being sick must have brought all that back." She sat up in the bed. "I knew it would. I knew he would think of her. I think about her now all the time too. I dream about it."

She told me about how one day Gladys was in the bed, resting, when the younger kids went off to school. When they got home, she had gone to the sanitarium. They never saw her alive again. "They didn't explain. We just put it all together. They burned her bed sheets, her clothes and toys. Anything she touched. Nobody could play with us. Nobody could come over. It was an epidemic. People were scared to let their kids play with us." She wiped her eyes. "He was the one who came home and told us. He could hardly talk."

"So answer me. Could you survive? If it was me?"

She looked at me for a long time. The thought of living through that, even if I was an adult child, shook her. She was caught between her memories of the death of a child a million years ago, and the thought that it could have been me in the bed now. "No. I could not."

TWENTY-EIGHT

After my initial calls, the news spread quickly. We were bombarded with notes from prayer groups, get-well cards, and UPS boxes bearing comfy cotton nightgowns with matching bathrobes.

Not a day passed that didn't yield a beautiful, handwritten letter of inspiration and hope from an old friend. *You can beat this thing. Never give up. God says when it's over, not doctors.* Every day we heard from old family friends, new friends, and people that we didn't know very well at all. But for Mother, there was something major missing. When the mail came and I read it to her, she'd ask, "Is that all? Are you sure there's not something else?"

She was looking for a note or a call from Katherine, one of the "Girls." After more than fifty years of friendship, they had had a falling out, and we hadn't heard a word from her since Mother moved to Las Vegas.

"Tell me what happened," I asked. If I could understand what had happened, then I could try to help fix it.

"I don't know what happened," she said. "I honestly don't know."

It just didn't make sense. How could two people who had been through everything together, like sisters, just drop out of each other's lives, especially at a time like this?

"It's crazy, you know. You should let me call her. You need to talk to her."

"No," she said. "If she wanted to talk to me—"

"I can't believe that she doesn't want to talk to you. How could she not?" I asked.

"I don't care. I don't want you to call her. She knows where to find me."

I was in a heck of a fix, not sure if she was just saying that she didn't want me to call, but secretly hoping that I'd call anyway. What if the thing that had come between them was horrible and couldn't be repaired?

"Don't you find it funny how this is happening all over again? Just like before?"

"What?" she asked.

"Maybe the two of you have some family curse," I taunted her. But it was true. Lightning was striking twice. My mother's mother—my grandmother—and Katherine's mother had been best friends. They'd seen each other through births and deaths and disappointments. One day, when they were in their seventies, they stopped speaking to each other. It was odd for all of us, especially my mother and Katherine. Many attempts were made on both sides to mend the friendship, until as suddenly and as mysteriously as it had started, the rift was repaired. They were back to sitting in their kitchens, talking on the phone for hours every single day.

"They made up a couple of months before Mother died," my mother remembered.

"Yes. But they were lucky. Grandma wasn't sick before. They made up without knowing what was ahead," I said. "I can't imagine what it would have been like if they'd never had the chance."

"Well, they did. Their friendship must have been different."

"I don't see the difference. Unless you think that they were closer because they went through more together."

"Nobody's been through more together than all of us. We shared more than we did with our own sisters," she said. And I knew that this was true. I can't ever remember a time when my mother's best girlfriends since childhood, Katherine, Gussie, Mildred, Josephine, Imogene, and Grace, weren't a part of my life.

It was Katherine who stepped in as wedding planner when Darnay and I got married. She was the thin line that kept Mother and me from killing each other over dresses, invitations, and flowers.

"I'm going to call her, Ma."

"No, you won't. I mean it."

But I lost my nerve and asked one of Mother's other girl-friends to do it. "I am sure they need to talk. You can ask. I can't," I said. Then I waited. And I waited. They never had the chance to talk.

TWENTY-NINE

The call that did come was from a woman named Claire, who had been assigned to be our hospice nurse. "I'd like to come by and meet Earline and your family today, if that's all right with you," she said.

It wasn't all right. Not at all. I didn't want to meet her. I didn't want her to get to know us. I felt about her the same way that Mother had felt about Ginger, but I hadn't even seen her yet. I was afraid of her. You only meet the hospice nurse when somebody is going to die.

"I'm not sure today is a good day. Maybe we can get together some other time. Mother isn't up to it today," I lied. She was having a pretty good day, and I didn't want the appearance of the angel of death/hospice nurse to change that.

"You're her daughter, right? Andrea, is it?"

"Yes," I said.

"Let me come today. Maybe I can help. If she's having a bad day, I might be able to help." Her voice was honest and sincere.

I believed her for a minute. Maybe she could help. After all, outside of Darnay, she was the only person in this whole ordeal, since Ginger, who had really offered to help. So I agreed and then went up and prepared Mother for her visit.

When she arrived, I was struck by how normal she looked for someone who had that kind of job. I was expecting a dark-haired ghoul with a widow's peak and long black fingernails. But she was crisp and clear-eyed, her perfect page boy held back from her face with a suede headband. They say that many serial killers look normal. What if I was inviting some fresh-faced, well-scrubbed ax murderer into our home? I immediately thought that I should ask her for references, but then I decided that Claire's client base never lived long enough to give them.

"I'm not going to lie to either of you. The truth is that my patients die," she said after I introduced her to Mother. She carefully and thoroughly described her role in this dying process and what we could expect. "My job isn't to help you get well. My job is to help you and your family face death with dignity."

Her words made me wince. Saying "death" in front of someone who was dying just sounded rude. But I had to get used to the fact that it wasn't rude. The goal of hospice, as she explained it, was to deal with death and dying in the most direct way.

"Once you face it and accept where you are, and set up systems by making your wishes known, then there are fewer things to fear. That's where the fear is, with the unknown."

I thought about Ginger again, and how Mother had hated her. Ginger had represented death, though she was a get-well nurse. But to my surprise, Mother was open to everything Claire said. "Will it hurt? Will I have a lot of pain?" she asked.

"I can't promise you that you won't have pain, but we are going to manage the pain. You just have to make sure you stay on top of it. Tell Andrea or me when you are feeling uncomfortable. We won't know unless you tell us," she said. She was kind, but she was clear and direct. She didn't pull back, and she didn't talk to Mother as if she was describing things out of a story-book.

She carefully went over the things we needed to know. She explained the prescriptions the doctor had ordered. She described the things she could do for us and the things she couldn't. She told us when she would visit and gave us phone numbers and instructions for when she was not around. It was a lot to take in.

"Remember, I am here to help you through your dying process. I'm not here to speed it up or slow it down. We do not provide assisted-suicide services." Mother nodded. Michigan had been a hotbed of end-of-life issues since Dr. Jack Kervorkian had made assisted suicide an ethical minefield.

"Is it true that he does it in a van, and then leaves them in the parking lot at the mall?" Mother asked. It was the one question that Claire never answered. My guess was that the hospice nurses had been instructed not to address Dr. Jack, as he is called here. Mother looked at me for affirmation. I had heard the stories too, but I just shrugged. Was that who she wanted me to call if she got to be "a vegetable"?

We signed a pack of papers—consent forms, liability forms, insurance papers, powers of attorney. Then she signed a living will that gave me the power to act on her behalf with doctors and hospitals in the event that she was not able to make her own wishes known.

"Should her husband sign it?" Claire asked, looking from Mother to me, and back to Mother again.

"No," Mother said. "No."

After everything was signed, Claire asked me to leave them alone for a bit. "If you don't mind?"

I did mind. I minded very much. I got a case of attitude, big time. She didn't know my mother. She didn't know me. How was she going to walk into my house and start telling me to leave the room? Oh no. How did she know that Mother wanted to be alone with her anyway? I folded my arms across my chest, and leaned against the wall, steadfast.

"It's okay, Ann. Go make some tea or something," Mother said, far more comfortable with Claire's presence than I was. Maybe she was closer to acceptance than I was. Maybe I still was prepared to fight.

I squinted at Claire hard, wanting her to know that I wouldn't hesitate to clean her clock if she hurt my mother. Then I spun around and left, all huffed up. What did they have to talk about that I couldn't hear? I had been there since day one. Were they talking about me? I went down to the kitchen, mumbling the whole time, and made some lemonade to offer Claire when they were done with their secret meeting.

They were up there about a half hour. Sometimes I would hear my mother howl with laughter. Sometimes I would hear Claire say, "It's always all right to cry." When I heard her say that, I started to rush upstairs, to the rescue. As I got to the steps, there was Claire, with her bag, and her folders, coming down.

I tried to walk around her to go up and make sure that Mother was doing okay. But she blocked me, put her hands gently on my shoulders and turned me around. "She needs a little time to process everything. Let's get something cold to drink and talk," she said. "Your mother's fine. Really."

We went into the breakfast room, then I brought two tall, ice-filled glasses of lemonade from the kitchen.

"Your mother is an amazing woman," Claire said, and reached out to touch my hand.

I bet you say that to all the girls, I thought. Then I looked into her eyes. They were warm caramel, unflinching. They demanded to be believed. I knew it then. She was there to help. She would help us. "She is something, huh?"

She took a long sip of her drink and nodded. She was an ice chewer like me. We crunched and talked. "She thinks the sun rises and sets on you and your family," Claire said.

"'Where is your stepfather in all of this?' Claire asked. I asked your mother, and she said, 'He's around.'" She looked to me for the truth.

"She's right. He is around. But he's not exactly an active participant," I said, trying hard to be on my best behavior, not wanting to air dirty laundry or speak unkindly of him. It was funny. In all the calls I had to make, nobody asked how John was doing or how he was holding up. I didn't have to lie or sound angry or resentful. Nobody wanted to know. This moment was the first time that anybody had asked about him in a long time. "He's having a hard time getting his arms around all this, I suppose."

She brought the pitcher to the table, topping off both our glasses. "I see that sometimes. Everybody handles death differently. It doesn't make them bad people. It just means that some people are not able to handle it. So they don't. They just shut down. Some of them go away."

"Well, that's just ducky. Some people get a chance to bail, leaving the rest of us to dog-paddle around in hell," I said.

"Come on now, even if he was here rolling up his sleeves and being Florence Nightingale, you would still do what you're doing. It's about who you are, and from what I can see, about what she is to you."

I sat quietly. It was true. And the fact was, it was easier that he wasn't around. I thought about what she'd said. "You see that? People do that? They just run away?" I had thought that family dysfunction was at the root of our situation.

She nodded. "In fact, some people stay so deep in denial that they don't even speak to me when I come to their houses. They see me every day, caring for their loved ones, and they never talk to me. Some are downright nasty to me," she said. "Because death is too scary. Some don't even believe that their husband or wife is going to die until after they're dead."

"God, how do you do this work? It sounds like a really horrible job to me," I said, then felt bad about saying it. "Sorry."

She shook her head. "No apology necessary. A lot of people think it's a weird thing to do. I do it because I love it, not because I can't find another job."

I asked what kept her from being depressed all the time. What kept her from being overwhelmed? I just had my mother to care for. Claire had a caseload of fifteen patients. She said that sadly; many of them would probably be gone by the end of the summer.

It wasn't lost on me that my mother was one of her caseload. Would she be gone by the end of the summer? My heart hurt again. My eyes stung.

"My work isn't depressing. Sometimes it's sad. But it's not depressing because I know that I am helping someone to let go." Her face lit up in a way that you wouldn't expect for a death worker. "People desperately need what I do. It used to be that everybody died at home, around loved ones who took care of them until the very end. But now, it's more complex. People work. They're spread out all over the country. Sometimes there is no extended family to pitch in."

"Have you always been a nurse?" I asked.

She nodded again, crunching more ice. "I worked in a hospital. Then when we started our family, I decided to be a stay-at-home mom."

I walked into the kitchen and brought back a basket of banana-nut muffins that I had made, along with some soft butter and plates. She took one and let out a sigh as she bit into it. "Oh, man, these are still warm," she said.

As we talked, we lost track of how many muffins we ate. I asked her how many kids she and her husband had.

"One, now," she answered. "We had a little girl, Louisa. We called her Lou Lou." She slathered a muffin with butter. "She was five when she was diagnosed with a rare form of blood cancer. She died."

The room stopped when she said this. She never took her eyes off me.

"I can't imagine," I said. "Weren't you angry?"

"There is nothing worse than losing a child. There is nothing, nothing that happens that's worse than the pain of going in your child's room and knowing that she's not there because she's dead. I couldn't get out of bed. I stopped talking."

I tried to visualize her with her thick brown hair tangled and matted, in dirty pajamas, with a streaky face and swollen eyes. I couldn't because she was so perfectly put together. But I could hear my grandfather's voice just days before as he'd talked about the pain of running to the sanitarium to see Gladys one more time, and getting there too late. Then I could see Claire coming undone one stitch at a time.

"How did you get through it?" I asked. If she had made it through the loss of Lou Lou, then maybe I could survive what I couldn't see now. I needed to know how she did it. I was living one day at a time because I had no choice. My mother needed me. I was anticipating falling apart once there wasn't someone who was so dependent on me. The kids had both Darnay and me, but my mother had just me.

"I went back to work to make some sense out of what happened to Lou Lou. I got sick and tired of being sick and tired." She never looked off into space the way I did when something became too much to talk or think about.

"Claire, how do you keep from getting attached to them? How do you do it every day?"

She told me that she did get attached. "Like now. I already like Earline. In those few minutes we spent alone, she told me some very personal things about herself."

Thinking about Ginger again, I found it hard to believe that my mother had told her anything real about herself. "What do you know about her?"

"Well. When I asked her what I could do to help her make the transition more easily, she talked about the pain. Her biggest fear is being in pain." She was silent for a minute, then added, "That's not right. It's her second-biggest fear."

"What was it then?"

"She is worried about you. She wants me to help you."

"Me?"

"Yes, she and I went over all the medical stuff. She knows that I will be here to help her in any way that I can. But she wasn't really worried about that. She said that she knew you would take care of her."

I could hardly see. My eyes filled thinking about Mother opening up and telling this stranger things that she hadn't been able to tell me.

"I suggested to Earline that maybe it was time for you two to sit down and talk about it," Claire said.

"What? The end?"

"If you want to," she said, taking a bite out of a muffin. "But you might want to talk about what happens after the end. That's what she's worried about. She wants to know that you'll be okay."

I hadn't even been able to make myself think about what would happen to me after she was gone. I couldn't touch that wound. I was going to deal with it when I had to. *After the end.*

"Ask her sometime what she's feeling and thinking. She's feeling and thinking a lot."

I'd been so busy caring for her physical needs and trying to make sure that she was comfortable that I hadn't spent a whole lot of time thinking about how she was dealing with her death. It was still too new. Maybe I didn't want to know that she might be scared. Maybe I couldn't handle it. I didn't even know how I felt. All I knew for sure was that I wanted the roller coaster to stop and let the two of us get off.

THIRTY

I couldn't grasp how Claire had managed during her daughter's illness and death. And I couldn't imagine making a career of watching people die, listening to their most intimate fears and secrets. Death seemed to be racing toward me and I was continually surprised that it could be just around the corner. It stunned me.

Something else surprised me and made me aware of the random selections of life. Almost immediately after the doctor declared that my mother's case was terminal and Claire came into our lives to help us wade through this unthinkable situation, people Mother and I knew started dying. People die every day, I know, but it was strange to watch her struggle through hospice care and try to get right with the inevitable, then answer the phone and get death news from home. Folks seemed to be dropping like flies. Friends of my grandparents. People my mother knew in high school and colleagues from her days at the telephone company.

Some of them had been sick with cancer, like Mother. I filtered that news out and never passed it on. Some died the way that old people do. But some were healthy, able-bodied working people with kids and full lives. Their deaths were flukes. Somebody ran a red light. Someone else fell down the steps and cracked her head wide open like a melon (my grandfather's description, not mine). Out of the blue, family friends caught colds that turned into pneumonia and then turned into comas.

As ghoulish as it sounds, there was something comforting about it. It redefined the word "terminal." We think of "terminal" cancer as the final frontier. Pack it up, Joe, that's all she wrote. Take a look around you and see all the people who will be here after you are gone. Say your good-byes.

Then suddenly people die who aren't supposed to die. Just when you get used to the predictability of it all, fate steps in and gives you something new to mull over. That month, we got word of no less than seven non-cancer deaths. At first, I filtered all death news, but then I started telling her and seeing how she reacted.

"Death is so sad, huh?" she'd say. But her face had something in it that I could never quite read. I know that she never relished anybody else's loss. But I am sure she became aware that she was outliving somebody she wasn't supposed to outlive.

We were watching television and a news report came on about a family of kids who had died in a fire. She became inconsolable. "How does that happen? Why do little kids die?" she asked. Lord knows, I didn't have the answer to that one.

"I think I've had a good life. I did a lot of stuff. I have you and Darnay and the kids. So how do people like me get up and little kids die?" she asked. It was a mystery to both of us. We could accept the sudden, sometimes random deaths of adults. But we both had a hard time coming to grips with the deaths of children.

She must have given as much thought to this question of fate as I had. "You just never know, huh? You could be walking down the street and somebody could drive by and shoot you."

I nodded. "You know, more people die of acts of violence than die of cancer." I tend to be a fount of bizarre information.

She processed this carefully. "So, am I terminal, really?"

How does one answer that? I had a hospital bed, a hospice nurse, and morphine pills to prove that she was terminal. But as we got news of folks having heart attacks, and choking on pieces of ham and having strokes, we started to look at it differently. "I guess 'terminal' is relative," I said, feeling pretty damn profound. There was a long pause while we took in the possibilities. It did make our own dismal little predicament less dire, somehow.

"So, if it really is relative, and we all are terminal, every last one of us, then you have to promise me that you will start living like it," she said.

"Like what?" I asked.

"Like life is precious. Like you do as much as you can while you can. Like every day matters."

"If you could do it over, what would you do differently?" I asked. I wanted to know what roads she would have taken or passed up if she had taken her own advice.

"A lot," she said. "I want you to live in a way that you won't be sitting somewhere with a shoe box full of regrets."

I thought about it and wondered what was in her shoe box full of regrets. Marrying John? Spending her whole life in Gary? The career choices she'd made?

"If you had to do it differently, would you still have had me?" I looked up at the picture of the young woman with the fresh press and curl and the crisp white blouse, holding the happily overdressed baby. How hard it must have been for her to be unmarried and pregnant in 1956. To hold her head up and teach me to hold my head up too. What would her life have been like if she hadn't gotten pregnant? What would she have been like if she had given me up for adoption or not had me at all?

She looked surprised, puzzled that I could think it. "Oh, Baby. I have never regretted that. Never that."

She grabbed my hand. "You do know that?"

"I do."

"So I want you to go off and live life. No regrets. For me."

I was thinking about what I would do differently and how I would make changes. I had put a lot of things on the back burner over the years. I could even say that I had been chasing the wrong goals. If I had to learn a lesson, maybe this was it. Maybe this was the big lesson.

"So are you going to do it? It's important to me to know that you are going to do it." She was so intent that I thought I was supposed to jump up and do something right then.

"Start now? You want me to do it now?" I didn't even know where to start. Then it dawned on me. "I do have something I want to do, but I need to ask you if it's okay.

"When this is all over, I don't want to take your role in the family. I don't want to be the fix-it girl. I don't want to be the peacemaker. I want to put John's ass in his car and send him back home. I want to say no to family drama. Okay?"

"You know how you asked me what I would do differently? Some of the things you just said." She smiled. "Sounds to me like you've got your plan. Now you just have to live it."

THIRTY-ONE

Things got unpredictable. There were good days and bad. The good ones were pain-free. Mother could take a shower and enjoy the warmer days on the screened-in porch. The bad days were like trying to blow out one of those trick candles. The good days were gifts. We treasured them and tried hard not to let anything keep us from enjoying them.

As the energy in the house began to intensify, so did Nicole's dramatic demands to be the center of each and every moment. Unfortunately for Miss Nicole, the only person who had the time or inclination to continue to treat her as if she were the Queen of Life was my mother, and she was dying, some days too weak or depressed to get out of bed.

We didn't do a great job of explaining what was going on to either of the children; we really didn't know how. And we kept putting it off.

For the most part, it didn't seem to be on Christopher's radar much, but Nicole knew that Granny had been very sick and took medicine that was so strong it made her hair fall out.

Granny's bed had buttons and lights and moved up and down like an amusement-park ride. A strange lady came around to take care of her. Papa John was at our house more. People came to see Granny looking happy, and they left looking sad.

Nicole also figured out that her own mother, who on the best of days, when she was not filling prescriptions, or putting pain patches on Granny, or taking phone calls, did not have the longest fuse for tantrums.

On one hot, muggy day, Nicole decided to put her landing gear down to see just how short the fuse was. She decided that if she ran away from home instead of taking a nap like I'd told her to do, the world would stop just to behold her wonder. Even if it didn't stop, it would almost certainly slow down long enough for my mother to placate her with a bundle of worthless crap and junk food.

Off she went in her white cotton panties with the pink and blue teddy bears. Not quietly, like a person who really wanted to get away. But screaming and shouting and crying like someone who wanted to be begged and promised a cold glass of extra-sweet lemonade and a trip to the mall—or whatever it took—to get her to come back in the house. But she had miscalculated. She had played her hand a little too hard for a little too long. Not unlike me, over thirty years ago.

But this time, my mother was hysterical. "You have to find her. She could get lost," she said. "Somebody could snatch her."

"Yeah, right. I am sure that someone is going to snatch a kid who is walking down the street in her drawers, cussing and swinging and yelling. She'd be such a welcome addition to any family. Especially the home of the devil."

"You have to go get her."

I was drowning and I couldn't swim. "Nobody is going to take her, and if they did, they'd bring her crazy little ass right back."

"But she's just a baby."

I needed air. I was feeling the squeeze of my mother's insistence. So I went to the window and pointed out at the yard. "Come here, Mother. I want you to see your baby."

There was Nicole, sitting behind the bushes sucking the life out of a cherry Popsicle. "Your baby is an evil forty-year-old midget. She even had sense enough to stop by the fridge and get a Popsicle for the road in case she had to wait it out for a while."

I looked down at my child, innocent and calm, with cherry juice running down her chin, her little breastless naked chest, and dripping on her underwear and legs. She was happy the way little children should be on summer days. Whatever the original battle was about, it had been forgotten in the wonder of the Popsicle. At least until she saw me. Then she started up again as if she had been taking a coffee break from hell-raising. As soon as I went out into the yard to get her, she started flailing and kicking.

My mother was up in the window, trying to calm her down, which I knew was pointless. "What are you doing to her, Ann?" she accused. "Come to Granny, Nicky. Granny will make it better."

"No. And shut up," Nicole snapped. Call the exorcist. Look out for those green peas.

That was the last straw. I grabbed her by the waistband of her underwear and up under her arms and dragged her into the house. She screamed and scratched, and bit, but to no avail. I was a mommy on a mission.

Nicole moved to her strategy of last resort. "Help, Granny. Help, she's killing me."

I took her up to my room, past my mother who was standing in the hall watching and crying. I sat on the bed and turned her over my knee and spanked her little butt.

"Granny, please. Make her stop."

"Ann, stop. Come here, Nicky."

"Mom, stay out of this. She's out of control."

Sweat poured down my face, into my eyes.

"Granny."

My mother appeared in the doorway. She was crying, doing what I had come to know as the Make You So Guilty You Want to Kill Yourself cry. She was very good at it. She faked labored breathing, holding on to the doors as if she was going to pass out.

"I can't take this. Stop." Mr. DeMille, she is ready for her close-up. Even Nicole stopped clowning and hollering long enough to watch. "Granny will protect you. Come here," Mother whined.

Nicole started to move toward her. I was through with both of them. I yanked my child back. "You sit there and you better not get up."

I walked quickly toward Mother. "A word, now." I escorted her back to her room, moving with her bony elbow in the cup of my hand. "Now."

When we got there, I ordered her to sit, where she started her big scene all over again. "I just couldn't take it. It makes me so upset and nervous. I can't take it."

"Ma, I saw that episode of *Sanford and Son*. Forget it."

She blinked as if she truly had been found out.

"You are going to leave me. I can't do a damn thing about it. We can't stop it." I was tight and controlled, talking slower and more thoughtfully than normal. But there was no doubt that the control came from anger. I'd had enough.

"Unless you are planning on taking Baby Cruella there with you when you go, you better straighten up. All you're doing when you rescue her is leaving me with a bigger mess than I started with. There is not a soul who is going to do that for her when you leave here."

Tears poured and she rubbed her face as if she had been slapped.

"Mother, when all this is over, I have to be the one to glue us back together again. You'll be in heaven playing slot machines and drinking beer. You have to stop."

"But—"

"But, hell. You thought you were playing me once again. You thought you were saving her. You were not."

So she had played her final scene. I knew it would come to this. "I just can't stand to see her so unhappy. If it has to be like this," she said, wiping her eyes and looking up to the heavens, "then just take me back to my apartment." There has never been a sadder face put on a human.

I wasn't buying. Seen it, lived it. "Okay, Mom. Hate to see you go."

The expression on her face changed to panic. "What?"

I got her overnight bag out of the closet, and went about packing up her stuff. "You said you wanted to go home. Let's go."

"You'd put me out?"

"No. I am just taking you home. You said that you couldn't live with the rules of my house, for my kids. You have a house. Go there."

"But . . ." This was not going as she'd planned. I could almost see her mind working. She had backed herself into a bit of a corner.

"I will either take you, or you can have John come get you, if you can find him." Then I walked out of the room. "I am going to finish with Nicole, and when I come back, you can tell me what you have decided."

When I opened the door to my room, Nicole fell over. She'd had her ear pressed to the door to hear what was going on. My mother had quickly figured out that I meant business, and that I had probably lost my mind too. She regrouped nicely, walking past us and down the steps to get a cold pop. "Well, Nicky, looks like it's every man for himself."

THIRTY-TWO

A few years before we moved to Lansing, I saw a story in the *Gary Post-Tribune* that almost made me lose my mind. It stayed with me, gnawing at something I couldn't identify until now.

A family I barely knew attended the same church we did, and moved to Baltimore two or three years before we moved away. I remember them as being nice, pillar-of-the-community people. The husband, a good deacon, always smiled and shook hands with everybody after services whether he knew them or not.

The son was a preteen growing out of his Sunday suits faster than his mother could buy them. He was a polite, shy kid who, when he stood at the front of the church to usher, had the tortured, strained look of someone who was being squeezed between the walls of adolescence and parentally enforced community service. I knew that look from my own clumsy, pimply adolescence.

And then there was the mother, who I can't even describe anymore. There was something back then, maybe her manner, or the way she talked, that reminded me so much of my own mother that when I try to picture her now, it's my mom's face I see.

The article in the paper told the awful story of how the father had died unexpectedly of a heart attack. The wife had wanted to have the funeral at his "church home" where all their friends were, but they had moved away before he died, and church policy said that a person couldn't be married or buried out of that church unless they were a card-carrying, dues-paying, altar-praying member at the time of their big event. According to the *Post Tribune,* the church ruled that because they had moved they were no longer members. Too bad, so sorry.

My own family knew this policy well. Darnay and I wanted to be married in the same church, but were denied because we were living in Detroit at the time, and had not officially joined the church, even though my mother had. The reverend agreed to marry us, but somewhere, anywhere, other than in his church.

Weddings were one thing, but it was impossible for me to believe as I read the story that the policy applied to funerals. Yet this poor, distraught woman, after her family's years and years of loyalty and sweat equity in that church, was being turned away.

I was in a buzzing tizzy over this. I called my mother in righteous indignation on behalf of the grieving woman, even though I couldn't remember what she looked like.

"Well, it is church policy," she said. It was clear that the congregation had been doing a fair amount of buzzing about it too. Mother just shook it off as if it were the mandated will of God.

"Where in the Bible does it say that if you buy the damn farm before you can get back and pay your dues that you have

to have your funeral in a bar, or in an aisle at the grocery store?"
I asked.

"He's not going to be buried in a bar. They are probably
going to do it at a funeral home. That's what they usually do
when this happens," she said.

"Usually happens? This happens a lot?"

She thought about it for a minute. "Oh, yeah. All the time.
But this is the first time it's happened to one of the old families,
I think."

"Well, that's crazy," I said. "I don't even want to belong to a
church that would have such a cruel and heartless policy." I was
ready to turn in my resignation as a member when my mother
reminded me . . .

"Technically, you don't belong to the church. You just go—
sometimes."

Days later, this story still nagged at me. I wrote the widow
several letters. Well, I wrote the same letter several different
ways. I didn't mail any of them because it sounded creepy to
send such passionate anger on someone else's behalf when your
letter started out, "You don't really know me, but . . ."

It was Darnay who reminded me that I didn't even go to
funerals. He thought it was senseless for me to get all worked
up about the funeral of a virtual stranger, me, a person who had
to be forced to go to my own grandmother's funeral.

"Well, I'd have gone to that one," I declared, wondering
why I was so obsessed.

"No, you wouldn't have," Mother said. "We have to drag
you to funerals with a leash and a collar. And those are people
you're related to." She was right. I wouldn't have gone. I was
floating on big principles, but I still wasn't sure why I felt that
the slight was personal.

Now, two years later, I figured out why. I was suddenly
entrusted with the execution of Mother's final arrangements.

She wanted to get everything all spelled out while she still could.

"I don't want you to have to answer to anybody, or have them force you to do what they want. If I tell you what I want, you can just do that," she said.

I squirmed at the concept, and started talking about the weather and the full moon.

"We need to have a plan, Ann."

"For what?" I asked.

"For the funeral."

I hadn't even thought about what happened after *the end*. In my mind, the end was, well, the end was the end. But it seemed that it was also the beginning of a whole lot of pomp and circumstance that I didn't have the energy to suffer through. Mother was right. I didn't like funerals.

At her insistence, I started a brand-spanking-new volume of Command Central. This one was called "Arrangements." The first task was to find a way to have the funeral at the church.

"I really want my service at the church, Ann," she said to me. "But remember what happened before."

I had no intention of denying her. I wasn't beyond begging, if I needed to. I rallied the wagons, or tried to. Everybody told me they would do what they could, but again and again they relayed the tale of the Baltimore widow to me. I asked my mother's friends back home to shake a tree for us, but all the answers came back the same, all through the grapevine. There was no official word.

Then one day a curt, exasperated little woman who announced herself as the church secretary called. "May I speak to Earline?"

Mother took the call. She didn't say much. She nodded. She listened. She dabbed her eyes with tissue. "I understand. I understand."

I wrote down a bargaining chip on a pad of paper and

pushed it in front of her. She asked the woman, "What would happen if I made a generous donation, or paid back dues, now? While I'm still alive?"

Back payments, reparations, overdue church support; it happens in child-support cases all the time. It sounded good when I thought it up, but listening to her, the request sounded more like groveling, or a sleazy bribe. It didn't even help. The answer was still no. More precisely, the answer was yes and no. Yes, of course they would be happy to accept a generous donation. No, there would be no funeral at the church.

A day later, a tiny concession came by way of another phone call from the church secretary. "This is what we have," she said. "The reverend is willing to perform the service, when the time comes, of course, but not in the church—one of the memorial rooms at the funeral home, perhaps."

"That's very generous. I'm sure that Mother will be delighted," I said as I choked on another one of those little lies I had to tell to get us what we needed. Then she offered me the church's new banquet hall for the repast, as long as we used the church's caterers, "of course." We came to an agreement, but I didn't understand why it was okay to have a dinner for the dearly departed nonmember at the church, but not the service itself.

After the church secretary hung up, I asked, "Ma, why do people even have those dinners? It's strange. I'm not going to want to be bothered with people after the service."

"You have to. It's customary and proper. It's what people do."

"Okay, I'll set it up, but do I have to go? I'll make the arrangements, pay for the food and flowers, tip the caterers, and then disappear."

The look on her face told me that I was going to arrange, write checks, attend, and be appropriately charming throughout the whole entire day. Or else.

THIRTY-THREE

"I want Darnay," Mother announced. It hadn't been a great day. We'd spent a lot of time trying to work with the pain, which was getting more intense and requiring more medication. So after a hard afternoon, she was exhausted, but got it in her head that she wouldn't rest until she saw him. "When he comes home from work, I need to talk to him."

I wondered what she was going to say to him.

"Is there something that I can help you with?" I asked.

"No. I just want my son-in-law. Tell him I need to talk to him."

When he got home, he changed into his golf clothes and we went into her room. She was in the bed, dozing and watching television as usual. "I've been waiting for you," she said. Her face lit up for the first time that day.

He pulled up the chair next to the bed. I stood in the doorway waiting to see what would happen next, trying to be as invisible as possible. But I was dismissed. "I want to talk to

Darnay . . . alone," she said, her voice firm. "Shut the door behind you, and don't be out there listening at the door. I want to have a little chat with my son-in-law."

To keep from going crazy with curiosity, I went downstairs to start dinner. About twenty minutes later, Darnay came down, crying so hard that it took a while to calm him down.

"What did she say to you?" I said, standing over him and rubbing his shoulders. "What on earth did she say to get you so worked up?"

He looked up and said, "Thank you." He wiped his eyes. "She wanted to tell me thank you."

THIRTY-FOUR

Planning a funeral, I found, was a lot like planning a wedding. It had all the same stresses of picking the right flowers and music. What would the star of the day wear? What scripture should be read? Would there be a candle-lighting ceremony? Who would be the pallbearers? Limos from the funeral home for the family, or cars?

Once the big question of where it would be held was taken care of, Mother and I got busy making all the other arrangements together. We talked about what she wanted, I wrote it down, and then got ready to make the calls.

"I'll be right back. I think we need a little help here," I said, and returned with a rum and Coke with a twist of lime and lots of ice for me, and the ten o'clock morphine pill for Mother. Not used to drinking in the morning, I also brought up some potato chips and green onion dip.

Mother looked over her glasses at me as I took a long swallow before making the first call. "Hell, if I live much longer," she said, "you're going to end up in Betty Ford." Then she chased down her pill with cold water.

"Well, Miss, if you live much longer, you *too* will be in Betty Ford, right along with me." We giggled. It was kind of ridiculous. By the time I got the undertaker in Gary on the phone, we were both pretty blitzed.

"My mother and I need to arrange a memorial service . . ."

"My deepest regrets," the voice said on the other end. "When would you like the service?"

I covered the receiver, but not very well. "She wants to know when we want to have it."

"We don't know," she whispered, and I repeated.

"You don't know?" The woman seemed surprised.

"Uh-unh. We just want to get everything all set up," I said, taking another sip of my drink, then sucking the juice out of the lime.

"Who is the deceased?" the lady asked.

"My mother. Her name is Earline Comer Terry."

"Oh, I knew her. I'm so sorry to hear it. What did she die of?"

"Ovarian cancer."

"What's she saying?" Mother wanted to know. Where were speakerphones when you needed them?

"She wants to know cause of death," I said to Mother, my hand over the phone again, whispering, but loudly.

"When did she die, if I may ask?" the lady interrupted.

"You can ask, but she's not dead yet. Do you want to talk to her?" From the long pause on the other end, I could tell that pre-planning was still a new thing in Gary. And I am sure that to an outside observer we were having way too much fun, but we had no choice. It was the only way we were going to get through it. We had to pretend that we weren't planning the good-bye. We had to pretend that we were party girls. I don't think I could have done it any other way, and I don't think she could have either.

I explained our situation so that the woman wouldn't think it was some drunken prank call. I told her about the reverend and the church arrangements, and that we were doing hospice care. I said everything had been decided.

Then Mother's morphine must have kicked in, big time. "Tell them I don't want to look like death warmed over," she said. "If I start to look bad, then I want to be cremated." She was so loud that I didn't have to repeat it.

"Please tell your mother that we are artists, and we can work wonders," the lady said, and I repeated it.

"Nope. I have seen some people who didn't look like themselves. They looked like shit. I don't want to look like shit. Just cremate me if I have to look all sunk in," Mother said. Then she started telling this awful story about a woman she knew who had been handled by said funeral home. "They should have just put a grocery bag on her head. It would have been better for everyone."

"Ma, I'm sure if the woman looked bad, she probably was unattractive before. They probably did the best they could," I said. The lady on the phone in Gary tried to get a word in edgewise, but we had all but forgotten that she was there.

"And that dress. If you put some crap like that on me, I'm coming back to haunt everybody." This tickled her. It tickled me too. But the woman on the phone was so flustered she suggested that we call her back when our plans and dates were firm, then she hung up.

We laughed and then we cried. It dawned on us that this wasn't some party with pretty music. It was death. Claire came in and found me on the floor sobbing, and Mother in the bed, begging me to stop. "I couldn't stand it if you fell apart."

Claire took the glass from me, smelled it, and asked what had happened. I heard Mother say, "I think I've decided on cremation."

THIRTY-FIVE

I'd have liked to shut out the rest of the world because there was so much to deal with. Mother was getting more fragile every day, for the most part only venturing out of the bed to go to the bathroom down the hall. She'd occasionally come downstairs, but her visits to the screened-in porch or the living room were rare. Our days were all about medicines and nurses and momentary pain crises. So the idea of being overrun with visitors who wanted to say a last good-bye did not appeal to me.

It was Darnay who convinced me that it was important to let the people who wanted to come and see her do so. "They don't want to be entertained, they just want to be with her. You can't cheat people of the opportunity to say good-bye."

He was right, but convincing Mother that he was right was not easy. She wasn't crazy about friends and relatives seeing her so thin and frail, so clearly sick. "I don't want people remembering me looking like this," she said.

"I think that people see who you are, and not what you look like on any one day. But I'll go out and get you some really pretty nightgowns, or you could wear some of the ones that you got from your friends," I said.

"Will you give me a manicure?" she asked, holding out her hands for me to examine.

"Of course, if you want one."

At that, she agreed to let visitors come. We asked that most of them just come up for a day trip; I couldn't really accommodate a houseful of overnight guests. And to my surprise, it was a big lift for all of us. I enjoyed preparing nice meals for our guests. I liked having people who would never have come up to Lansing, Michigan, for any other reason come to my house and see that I was living like a big girl.

Every day a friend would arrive and my mother would hold court as lady of the house. Even if she'd had a sleepless, painful night, she was able to put on a game face the next morning and spend a little time with her siblings and their children and other friends who wanted to see her.

My friend Candice, who had been my maid-of-honor, came with her teenage son, Michael, who delighted the children with rough-and-tumble play. Candice had lost her own mother to breast cancer a few years before. I remember the day she'd called to tell me that her mother had died. It was one of those moments that telegraphed a chill, an ache, and said, "Pay very close attention. This could happen to you." And years later, it did.

THIRTY-SIX

When I was in Las Vegas, I met a guy who was a Barbie artist. He made up their faces with tiny brushes, restyled their hair, and made glamorous gowns for them to wear. He showed me how to do it, and when I got home, I went to the craft store and got my own supplies. It took my mind off things for a bit. I sat quietly and did one doll after the other in between answering calls from concerned relatives, giving out meds, and running errands. It was such a distraction. Mother sat watching me, smiling, content that I had something to hang on to.

"You sit there with those dolls like you used to do when you were little."

But she worried that I never got out. "Instead of buying dolls, maybe you should go out and buy yourself something. Go shopping. Have lunch."

I didn't want to buy myself anything. I didn't have anybody else to have lunch with, and I couldn't stand to be away from her for too long. I was afraid that the moment I left, she would die, alone.

Then one day she insisted. "You have to get some air. You have to go out and do nothing. I'm worried about you."

Claire agreed. "You can't take care of her or the kids if you don't take care of yourself."

They had already arranged for John to come and sit with her for a couple of hours while I went out. He showed up right on cue and I explained the medication schedule to him, and wrote it down. Claire handed me my purse and keys and walked me to the car.

"Have fun," Mother said as she waved me off. "I'll be fine."

So I set off to have fun, whatever that was, but mostly I marked time until I could come home.

ↄ℈

When I got back from my excursion, three hours later, Claire's car was in the drive. I ran in the house and found John in tears in Mother's room, trying to explain what had happened. Claire was rubbing his shoulder, consoling him. "It's okay. It's okay."

My mother had a goofy, dazed look on her face. "Hi, Baby. Did you have fun?" Her speech was slurred.

I was so mad that I was seeing stars. "What the hell did you do to her? What—"

Claire took me by my arm and led me out into the hall. "It's okay. Apparently he got confused on the meds when she started experiencing more pain. He lost count. Then he panicked and called me."

"He lost count? It was written down. What do you mean?"

"I think he gave her too many pills. But it's okay."

I had left him with her. I figured he could do this one little thing. "Claire, get him out of here."

"Look, this isn't what we wanted to have happen," Claire said. "But it isn't awful either."

I didn't understand why this wasn't awful.

"Between you and me, what's the worst that could have happened?" she whispered. "She could have died, which she's going to do anyway."

She was right, but it was just the whole idea of him screwing up. When I came back in the room, he was still babbling and apologizing. "Go home," I said. "Get some rest and come back tomorrow. Or the next day." As a charitable footnote I said, "It wasn't your fault. It will be okay." *Just get out.*

Claire showed him out, and tried to calm him down. I could hear her reassuring him that he had done a fine job, given the circumstances. I put all of my attention on my mother. "What happened here?"

"I scared him. He was scared to death to be here with me by himself. So I scared him even worse." She winked.

"I howled and hollered. He'd give me a pill. I cried and he'd give me a pill. You should have seen him. He got all flustered and lost count."

"But you know the schedule. Why did you do that? You could have overdosed."

"Because I could," she said and then dozed off for just a matter of seconds. "You should have seen him. It was a hoot."

"But, Ma, you could have killed yourself." My worse fear as of late was that one day the pain would get to be too much for her and she would beg me to help her end her suffering. Every day that we got through without that request was a blessing to me. But to think that through some stupid slipup she could have gone made my face tighten.

She waved it off. "If I had, then he would have thought he did it. It would have served him right." This was a woman you didn't want to cross.

"Well, I can't leave him alone with you again. He doesn't know how to take care of you."

She leaned in and gestured for me to come closer. She whispered, "He never did, Baby. He never did." With that she started snoring.

⌁

The next day, at eight A.M., when I went in to check on her, she was still sound asleep. At least I thought she was. Every time I saw her sleeping these days, I'd move in close and watch to see if her chest moved. Sometimes I'd stick a little hand mirror under her nose to see if it would fog up. I must have seen that done in an old movie.

She caught me doing this once and said, "I used to watch you like that when you were a baby." She smiled at me as if she were looking at her fuzzy-headed six-month-old.

I remembered the day we brought Nicole home from the hospital. I held her in my arms, not trusting her to a car seat. I stroked her cheek in wonder that something so tiny and beautiful could have come out of me. Then I noticed that she didn't seem to be breathing. "Pull over," I cried to Darnay, "I think we killed her." He took two lanes to get over to the side of the road. We patted her, and kissed her tiny fingers. We called her name. But she didn't move. We were both in tears. My mother had said that maybe I wasn't responsible enough to have a baby, although I was two years older than she was when she had me. And it seemed at that moment that she was right. Somehow I had managed to kill my baby two seconds off the maternity floor.

Darnay took off, back to the hospital. As we got to the emergency-room door, Nicole let out a big, loud yawn, twisted her head from left to right, and went back to sleep.

But now, Mother didn't yawn. She didn't look up at me and smile. She just slept. I called Claire, panicked.

"She's never not gotten up. I don't think she's dead, but—"

Claire was a pro at this dying stuff. She calmly gave directions, as if she were guiding me through making brownies, but I was freaked and I wanted her to be too.

"Remember your hospice instructions. Don't call 911 or the hospital. That's important."

It had sounded like a good idea when we'd gone over it before. It had made sense not to prolong anything. But now it went against every reality I knew. If someone was in crisis, you called 911. "What if this is it, Claire?" There was silence on the other end.

One hour later, she arrived with medical bag in hand. I shot questions and she ignored them, going about all the things she knew she had to do. She checked Mother's pulse, put a stethoscope to her chest, put a digital thermometer in her ear, opened her eyes and flashed a light in them. And still Mother didn't wake up.

Finally, she looked at me and said, "This could be it."

"What do you mean, *it?*" I was angry and scared and tired. I was ill prepared for "it." All the talk we had done about letting go, and "being free," was just talk. Things were moving too fast. All of a sudden, Claire was the unwanted messenger. At this moment, when it seemed that Mother was floating out of my life, hospice was a bad idea. It was too logical, too detached. It was science. This was my mother and she was leaving me. It never occurred to me that death could come so quietly, although every morning I was surprised that she was still there.

"You don't mean that she's slipping away right now?" I looked down at Mother and rubbed her arm.

"No, not this second. But soon. Tonight. Tomorrow. She could be slipping into a little coma."

After Claire left, I sat down beside Mother. "Snore or do something, will you?" But she didn't. And for the first time in a long time, I had nothing to do. No pain patches to apply. No food to bring up and take back down again to eat for her after I got back in the kitchen. No small talk to make.

I used to be so afraid of losing her when I was a kid. I had friends who had lost parents. Car accidents, or in one instance, one's father killed his mother, and then turned the gun on himself. I picked up this thing while I was in Catholic school about the angel of death. The nuns said that the angel of death comes when you least expect it. So I trained myself to expect it all the time. It seemed to keep everybody safe, but the fear didn't go away. I used to worry when I was in college about the dreaded call in the middle of the night. But it never came.

Cancer didn't leave me with much, but it did give me a year to say all the things that people who get these shocking calls in the middle of the night never get to say. For the past year, I'd been saying them and doing them. Cancer gave me that. But it was happening too fast. There were still a million things that needed to be said.

Now, there was nobody in the room but the two of us. I found comfort in the fact that if she could hear me as she was slipping out the back door, she couldn't come back and thump me in the back of the head like she'd done at the soft-serve machine or put me under punishment for life. So I said them. And I imagined her answering me.

"I forgive you, Mom." I took her thin little hand and rubbed it. "I forgive you for smothering me."

"And I forgive you for being a willful, hardheaded child."

"And I forgive you for disliking my boyfriend to the point that I hung on to him four years too long just to prove to you that you were wrong about him," I said. "You were right. I hate it when you're right."

"I forgive you for being so stupid about him. He was an asshole and you knew it." I could have sworn I heard her say that.

"Well, I forgive you for not talking to me about sex, and men, and everything you thought I would run out and do if you told me about them," I said. "I could have saved myself a lot of hard lessons."

"No, you wouldn't have. You would have done them anyway. You did do them anyway."

I smiled and wiped my eyes. She was right. I would have.

"I forgive you for being such a loner," she said.

This pissed me off. My mother always conveniently forgot a key point. "I forgive you for turning me into a loner. What else was I going to be? Only children are loners, we survive that way."

"Whatever."

"Mom, I forgive you for undermining my motherhood. I had to arm-wrestle you every step of the way."

"Well, I guess that's what happened to me too, when you were little. You always thought of your grandmother as the real law and order. So I just wanted my chance, I guess." I think that was really true.

"Mom, I also want to thank you. For everything. Everything."

How could I have such a complete and complex conversation with someone who was somewhere between here and there? We sat quietly for some time.

"I do have one thing that I don't forgive you for. I can't." I was mad again. I hurt. I had a big, huge lump in my throat and a throbbing in my head. "I can't forgive you for dying. Don't die. Get up."

I walked back to bed and cried myself to sleep.

An hour later, I got up and went back into her room, knowing nothing had changed. And it hadn't. I didn't want to talk to her anymore. If she wasn't going to talk, then I wasn't either—so there!

Instead I moved things around. I stacked books, I dusted figurines. I opened blinds and closed them, then decided they should be opened.

I decided to turn on the television to break up that awful silence.

"Can I have a Pepsi, please?"

I looked closely at the television to see whose voice I'd heard.

I looked over at Mother, but she was exactly the way I'd left her, eyes closed, arms at her side. I had lost my mind. I was hearing voices. I shook my head, and kept fidgeting and fussing with things in the room.

"Ann, I really would like some cold pop." There it was again. I turned around and she was sitting up, smiling, yawning, rubbing her eyes.

"Ma, is that you?"

"No. It's somebody with a bad haircut who needs a cold pop, with lots of ice."

"What happened? I really thought you were—"

"Dead? No, not yet. Just overmedicated. Like sometimes when you're so sound asleep that you can't wake up."

I know my mouth was open and every time I tried to shut it, the wonder of the whole thing made it fly open again.

"Don't just stand there, I'm dying of thirst."

THIRTY-SEVEN

The next day Gussie, Frances, and her sister Mert drove up from Indiana to spend the day with Mother. I was worried that she wouldn't be up to visiting, but she insisted. We got her all spruced up, put a little makeup on her, and off she went to meet her guests.

I warned them when they arrived that the last few days had been rough, and I didn't know what to expect. "Yesterday I thought she was going to die. She wouldn't wake up." While I was whispering about her, she walked down the stairs by herself, which she hadn't done in a week.

We all held our breaths as she made it down one step, then the next. Darnay was standing by to catch her if she fell.

"Ma, let Darnay come get you," I begged.

"No, no. I can do it. I'm fine." Then she missed a step and took a tumble. Darnay caught her, swept her up, and carried her to the couch.

She thanked Darnay, and asked us to leave them alone. It was so quiet for a while. I wanted to peek in, but felt that they needed to have the time alone. The next thing I knew, they were laughing and talking, like old times. She sounded like her old self, telling little stories and catching up on all the Gary gossip.

When the visit was over, and I walked them to the car, I thanked them for giving her the best day that she'd had in a very long time. "I could almost believe that this isn't happening."

"Maybe it isn't," one said. "Maybe she'll fool everyone."

I hugged each one of them, then said, "I think we'll probably be seeing you next week." I didn't know why I said it, or how I knew. It wasn't just her best day in a long time; it would end up being her last good day ever.

After they got back home, Gussie called. I reported the latest on Mother's condition. I thanked her for being such a good friend to Mother and to me. "Your being here meant everything to her," I said.

In return, she said something that caught me off guard. "You are so grown up. I'm so proud of you."

I was thirty-six years old then. I had ten years of marriage under my belt. I had two kids and a mortgage. But it dawned on me that to them I would always be Earline's baby girl. I would always be the little girl in the photo on the fireplace mantel. And for the first time, it wasn't a burden. It was an honor.

THIRTY-EIGHT

The next day was our tenth wedding anniversary. Darnay and I had become so brittle and breakable from the constant flow of guests, lack of sleep, grief, and worry that we'd almost forgotten. Although we'd managed to stay strong through my mother's diagnosis and treatment, the flurry of visitors who needed to be entertained had taken a toll on us.

Right after the last guest left, Darnay mopped the hardwood floors in the living room and, without thinking, I walked across them while they were still wet and flopped down on the couch. He went ballistic. I went ballistic. Fortunately, somewhere in the moment we knew that it wasn't about the floors, or about each other. We were simply stretched too tight. It felt as if this would never end. Neither of us could remember what it was like to be in this house before cancer took over all our lives.

After a family goes through this, there is the tendency to nurture the romantic notion of how blissfully noble everyone involved has been. When you are living through it, there is no bliss, no nobility, and definitely no romance. If there is such a thing as a point when things get to be too much to bear, we had all reached it, or so we thought. As soon as I said, "It can't get any worse," something would happen that would let us know that we ain't seen nothing yet.

After he yelled at me for violating his floors, I stomped upstairs in tears. I swore I would never speak to him again as long as I lived. I went into Mother's room to give her her medicines. Going through the ritual of taking off her old pain patches and putting new ones on took my mind off how angry and hurt I was. We were using more patches each time, and we were running out of space on her little chest and arms to put them. Of course they weren't enough, so I counted out the variety of pills she had to take, including the morphine.

I didn't like the idea of her taking morphine, and I told Claire, "She could become an addict or something."

"Believe me, at this point, becoming an addict is the least of her problems," Claire said. "The goal is to keep her as comfortable as possible until she makes her transition."

I hated that saying—"makes her transition." What is she going to transition into? A butterfly? A bird? Am I going to come in the room one morning and find her gone and a dove in her place, perched on the bed rail? Is it going to fly away? Is that the transition?

Armed with Claire's assurance, I sorted out the pills, poured the water, and sat down on the edge of the bed. I made small talk. She nodded, or would say, "Okay," but for the most part said very little.

"Are you all right? I want to make sure that you aren't having any pain," I said.

She shook her head. "No pain now."

"You'd tell me if you were hurting, wouldn't you?"

"No pain." She looked at me with wide-eyed hopefulness. It scared me to have her place that kind of trust in my ability to make everything right.

Her look changed. Her head tilted to get a better look at me. "Crying?"

I had almost forgotten. "Yeah, Darnay pissed me off. I tracked his perfectly mopped floors."

She half-smiled and closed her eyes for a few seconds. I was still plotting ways to avoid ever sending a swinging syllable his way for the rest of my life while I prepared the rest of her pills.

I put the pills, some big, some small—about six or seven—in my hand, as I always did several times during the day. I usually handed them to her one at a time, and she would take one, drink some water, then get another one. Now, I held out my hand and she took all of them. My mind was somewhere else, and it never occurred to me that she would stuff them in her mouth and try to swallow them without water.

Her throat was so narrow that she couldn't move the bundle of pills and she couldn't cough them up. They just sat there, visible like the egg that had been swallowed whole by the snake.

I tried to get her to drink the water but it didn't help. She just coughed and spit up the water. I didn't know what to do. I was panicked, but she didn't understand what was happening, was not even aware that she was choking. Coughing and gagging were natural human reflexes, but her eyes said that she was so out of it, she didn't know what was going on.

"Oh, my God. Mama, spit up the pills."

I was afraid to hit her in the back to force the pills up. She was so fragile that I could easily have broken her ribs. I did the only thing I could think of. "Darnay, help. Help me."

He took the stairs two at a time, and within seconds appeared in the doorway.

"She's choking. Her pills," I said.

He didn't miss a beat. "Hold your arms up for me, Earline." He leaned her forward slightly and hit her firmly between the shoulders. Nothing happened at first. Then he did it again with a little more force. She gasped, gave a big cough, and then the pills came flying out of her mouth. He raised her up again. She smiled at him and said, "Water, please."

That night I couldn't get rid of the image of the pills trapped, gnarled in a ball in her throat. I would have cried, but I worried that if I didn't keep it together, I wouldn't be able to deal with whatever came next. But I thought about how nice it would be to start howling at the moon or running through the yard eating Popsicles in my underwear like Nicole. Or retreat into myself, naturally or drug-induced, like Mother had. I would have given anything not to be functional. Or responsible. Or so scared. Hell, none of those things was an option. So the only thing I could do, I did. I got one of the Barbies and crawled into bed. Darnay tucked me in. "Happy anniversary, Ann."

THIRTY-NINE

After the episode with the pills, everything started moving with lightning speed toward the end, and we all knew it. Even the kids had taken to avoiding Granny. They crawled past her door on all fours to get down the stairs without being spotted. It was getting pretty scary for them and for us.

Thank God for Claire, who was my daily guide through what was happening. She had a talent for explaining exactly what I was seeing and experiencing and always knew what to do next. I can't imagine what it would have been like to do that all alone.

In a lot of ways, it's like shutting down. Every day, every hour. No foods, no fluids, no mobility. One day Claire removed the IV. The next morning Mother just stopped talking. The only sounds she made were, "Owww, owww," which meant that she was uncomfortable in some way.

Staying on top of the pain, keeping it at bay for long, became nearly impossible. All I could do, as Claire said, was to "keep her comfortable," and I couldn't even do that right, feeling swallowed up by how I was failing her. It was agonizing for me. I couldn't keep her alive, and now I couldn't keep her from screaming out in pain. Her system was eating up everything I was giving her as fast as I could give it.

At first I could give her the pain meds in her hand. Of course, I got leery of giving her all the pills at once after they got caught in her throat. Claire brought over these little tools, sponges on the head of a lollipop stick, and eyedroppers. The sponges were to push the new pills, which didn't have to be swallowed, under her tongue. The eyedroppers were to give her bits of water, like a baby bird.

How far we had come in that year. Twelve months before, I was practicing the fine art of muffin making, thinking I might like to be a caterer when I grew up. Twelve months ago, I was thinking that I should get serious about writing if I could ever find anything important enough to say.

Now I was in charge of helping someone move toward the end of her life. Not just anyone, my mother. I was the temperature taker, the spiritual adviser, the companion, the morphine pusher. I laid on pain patches as if they were ceramic tile. There wasn't a single day that I didn't wonder what made me qualified to do such important work. There wasn't a day that I wasn't convinced I wasn't screwing it up. I wished someone would fire me, but there was nobody to take my place. *Such a big job for such a little girl, Mommy.*

"Owww, owww."

The rest of our lives happened somehow. I couldn't cook. I couldn't pick up the kids from day care. I took time out to shower only when Darnay was home. I couldn't work. If I left the room to go to the bathroom, when I got back, she was howling in pain.

On Monday, Claire taught me how to roll Mother from left

to right using a towel, how to clean her up and change the bed linen. She did it with such ease. And I paid attention, I swear. But on Tuesday, when I had to do it alone, with no help, I couldn't get the towel under her or flip her or roll her. She wouldn't budge. She just watched me and howled.

"Mama, I have to do this," I begged. "I have to do this." I moved from one side of the bed to the other, hoping that I could get some leverage. Her eyes followed me with great interest, but she was so out of it, she couldn't figure out what I was doing, or how to help me do it.

"Mama, can you just help me a little?" I asked. I had somehow managed to get the towel under her but had gotten my arm stuck. When I tried to move, she cried.

I finally wiggled free and called Claire's pager. I sat on the floor to catch my breath and rethink my strategy. When I got up to try one last time, I felt so frustrated and helpless that I started to cry.

"I can't do this anymore. I can't," I said as I took off my shoes, climbed in the bed, stood up, and bent over to try it again. "I can't do it. I can't keep you from hurting. I can't bathe you." I lost my footing and fell on her.

I got back up, straddled her, and bent over again, determined to get a good grip. When Claire arrived, I was standing up in the bed over Mother, crying uncontrollably.

Claire got me down and out of the bed. She sat me in the chair and knelt down.

"I'm sorry. I can't do this. I can't do hospice anymore. Hospice is not working. It's a nightmare," I said.

"Ohhh," Mother said.

Claire had a talent for bringing order to chaos even when there was no order to be had. She wiped my face with a tissue. "Listen to me. It will be okay, honest."

"It's not ever going to be okay," I said with the conviction of someone who was sure that life was going to be hell from this moment on. Hell for me, hell for my mother.

"We're at the end now. You're just exhausted, as well you should be. And this is hard, hard work," Claire said.

"Claire, I've thought about this. I need you to call the hospital. I need you to tell them that she's in crisis. Lie if you have to." I had her hand. "Tell them that she's having a seizure. I don't care. Whatever you need to say to get them to take care of her. I don't want her in pain anymore. I don't want to have to hurt her just to change the damn sheets."

She shook her head, then she took my face in her hands and made me look at her. It was like in the old movies when the straight man slaps the hysterical comic. It worked; I stopped babbling long enough to hear her out.

"If you call them to take her to the hospital, they will stabilize her, and then they will put her back in the ambulance and bring her right back here. She's going to be even more miserable if they keep picking her up and moving her back and forth."

Thinking about this possibility, I felt trapped.

"I also have to tell you that if you call the hospital to intervene, your hospice care stops when they bring her back. Hospice is support, not intervention," she said.

"What does that mean?" It sounded like I was being threatened.

"When they bring her back, it could mean that you will be all on your own, till the end," she said, hugging me now.

She got up and gave Mother some pain meds. "Earline, I'm going to take our girl downstairs and get her calm, okay?" she said. My mother didn't answer. She just watched. Always watching.

Claire took me by the hand and led me downstairs to the kitchen. She went to the refrigerator and got me some cold water. We sat at the kitchen table and she explained the next steps.

She was going to get an order for stronger pain medicine and have the pharmacy deliver it. Then she was going to get me a home health aide to come in once a day to change the sheets and sponge-bathe Mother. "See, you won't have to do that," she said.

I was on automatic pilot, far too drained to argue.

An hour later, the pharmacy brought in the big guns, mega morphine and a fresh supply of sponges on a stick. Then the home health nurse arrived, patted me on the shoulder, and went upstairs. I waited in the living room. I didn't want to be there when Mother started fighting the stranger. I covered my ears so I didn't have to hear her crying out.

Minutes later, the woman reappeared. "Couldn't handle it, huh?" I said, smirking.

"No, not at all. She's a sweetie. It was a piece of cake." She was all done. "I'll see you tomorrow," she said and was gone as quickly as she had come. One problem solved, one major problem with no real solution to go.

This stronger prescription for morphine seemed to make a difference for the first day, but I still needed to add the patches. The pain was a wild thing, out of control. The next day Claire said that we had reached the maximum strength without putting her into a coma. All that was left to do was give her what she needed, when she needed it. For three days it went on nonstop, every four hours, then every two hours. It wasn't long before I was pushing little pills in her mouth every single hour, because that's how often she cried out in pain. There was no training, no mental preparation, no previous on-the-job experience to call on. There was no peace, for her or for me.

FORTY

On Thursday morning, Claire arrived after Darnay had taken the kids to day camp and headed off to work. She took one look at me and knew that I hadn't slept in days.

My eyes didn't even blink anymore.

"How's your mom doing?" she asked.

"Well, she went for a spin in the car, and told me to tell you that she'll be right back." I hung my head. "Forgive me, just a little hospice humor." I hugged her.

"One day, when you get past this, I'll share some real hospice humor with you." She smiled. "I have some doozies, but you have to be in the right frame of mind to hear them." I wasn't in the right frame of mind to hear anything.

We went up to see Mother. She was making a new noise that had developed during the night. It was a raspy, guttural thing that a really good cough would fix. It rumbled around in her chest, fighting to get out.

"Death rattle," Claire announced. Death rattle? There ought to be a less direct, less common name for it. I was almost

215

offended that this thing was called a death rattle. It was one of the last stages. It should have had more grandeur, more dignity, more weight, more power, like the other cancer words.

"It sounds terrible, but it's not hurting her, honest," Claire said. Then she went about her work, checking her vitals with the stethoscope, taking her pulse, and flashing a little light in her eyes.

"Any time now," she said.

"How do you know? What changed?" I looked at my mother so closely. Did death look a certain way? Did my mother's death look different from my grandmother's? Her eyes were at half-mast, showing small bits of white. Her mouth was open, and that awful noise came out, that rattle. Her face was sunken. Her color was gone, replaced by a beige white. No eyebrows. No lashes. Who was this woman? Where was my mommy going?

"Her heartbeat has speeded up. It can't go on beating like that. Eventually, it will slow down, and then it will just stop," she said to me. Then she stroked the side of Mother's face. "It's okay. You can let go," she said to Mother.

"Can she hear you, hear us?" I asked.

"I think so. I'd like to think so." She took the stethoscope back out again and placed it on Mother's chest. Then she said, "Take her hand."

When Claire said that death was coming soon, I didn't think that soon meant immediately. But it did. I took her hand and told her that I loved her. I refused to cry. I wanted her to hear me, not my tears, not crying. I wanted her to hear me say good-bye. "I love you, Mommy."

The rattle stopped. Her eyes fluttered. She took a deep breath that made her chest rise and fall. Then it was done. I looked at Claire for confirmation. She nodded. I immediately dropped her hand and backed away from the bed.

"What's wrong? Are you afraid of her?" she asked. She had seen death and dead people so often that it was routine for her.

I wasn't afraid, but I was humbled. I was amazed. There were three people living and breathing in that room just minutes before. Now there were two. The parts of her that meant something to me, her soul and her spirit, were leaving the room, or changing form. As Claire liked to say, "transitioning."

I looked down at this body. Her body. It had failed her even more so than I had. It was all that was left. I knew that what I held inside me, which would always be there, had nothing to do with this beaten body. The things that mattered were still with me.

I had no feeling for this thing. It wasn't Mother. I didn't want to see it again. I left the room. "Not afraid, Claire. Just done."

There were calls to be made and things to be done. The first one was to meet with Claire in the bathroom. By law, we counted out the remaining morphine tablets. She logged them in her book, and then we flushed them. We wouldn't want the daughter to become an incurable dope head on her mother's pain meds, now would we?

Claire called the funeral home to come get the body. And I called the people I needed to call. The calls were brief. "It's me. It's over. I will see you tomorrow."

I heard John's car pull up at the usual time. I went downstairs to meet him at the door. "She's gone."

I got in bed with my clothes and tennis shoes on, still determined not to cry. There was too much to do and get through. Darnay came home in time to meet the people from the funeral home, so I didn't have to deal with them. He came in the room, sat on the bed, and held me. All I could say was, "My mommy is gone. My mommy is gone."

FORTY-ONE

That night I had my first sound sleep in a month. Nobody was going to forget that she couldn't get out of the bed and fall. Nobody was going to need a pain patch, or a morphine lollipop. Nobody was going to suffer that night, so I could sleep.

I got up the next morning and threw some things in a bag, and drove her car back to Gary. Darnay and the kids would join me later that evening. When I finally got to my grandfather's house, I wasn't sure how I was going to get through it all. I sat in the car, with the air conditioning blowing on me, watching people who had come to pay their respects file in and out of the house. What would happen if I just never went in? What would be the worst that could happen?

Then I started talking myself into it. *You can do this. You can do this. This is the last little thing you have to do. You just have to get through the next two days. That's all you have to do.* But it was much safer in the car.

I had rehearsed it all in my mind on the three-hour drive from Lansing to Gary. There would be so many questions.

People would ask, How is John? I'd say, *I don't know, haven't you seen him?* People would want to know if the end was terrible. I'd say, *It was.* They'd ask how I did it. I'd say, *One day at a time.* I'd say, *It was an honor.* I'd want to say, *Hell if I know,* but I wouldn't say that. Then I'd have to answer all the questions about the funeral and the cremation. Why so fast? Why cremation? Why didn't you ask me what I thought? That would take the most diplomacy.

None of it was getting done with me sitting in the car, listening to Patti LaBelle sing "You Are My Friend," so I took a deep breath, put on some lipstick, and got out. The first person I saw was my mother's friend Katherine, and it threw me off my mark. My heart beat fast. We looked at each other for a long time, each waiting for the other to speak.

"I didn't know she was so sick. I didn't know . . . ," Katherine said. "I didn't think she would . . ."

"Die?" There it was, out there. I was still getting used to saying it and feeling it. "She did. She died." And then I reached out and hugged her. Holding each other, crying together, made it real. I wanted to hold on to this moment and burn it in me. I didn't ever want to forget the lesson that there is never enough time to patch things up. We forget that the meter is always running and that sometimes the watch stops before we can make things right. Somebody leaves somebody else behind with awful pain. I wouldn't have traded places with Katherine then for anything in the world. I ached for her more than I did for myself.

"I wanted to call. I wanted to . . . ," I said, feeling that somehow it was my fault.

"You should have. I should have."

I didn't have to say that Mother needed her, that she really wanted to talk to her at the end. I knew that she felt it. In a few minutes, the people in the house spotted me with her, and started calling for me. Show time. The moment that we had alone on the tiny porch, with the last of the evening sun shining on us, holding hands, was about to be broken.

"She loved you," I said softly. "She truly loved you."

Katherine told me that she loved Mother too, which I had always known. What had happened between them in the end wasn't for me to judge. It was over. All that was left was the lifelong friendship.

Then she looked at me and I saw the same look in her eyes that I had seen almost ten years before, when she and my mother had come to inspect me just before I went down the aisle in my wedding dress. "And oh, she loved you too," she said.

FORTY-TWO

Over the next few days, my mouth moved, and I only hoped that what I said was appropriate. If the person I was talking to frowned, I'd backtrack and try to fix whatever I'd said. If they hugged me or cried, then I knew I had done a good job.

It was the Girlfriends who saved me. They closed ranks around me, shielding me from everybody else's agendas and running interference, just like Darnay.

They understood that I was doing the best I could with what I had been given, and that it was all falling on me. They knew that I had already paid my dues. Where everyone had been surprised by her "sudden illness," it was as much a part of me as my own arms, my own legs, my own breathing.

Somehow they seemed to know what I meant when I said that I'd had my first real night's sleep in a week on the night after Mother died. They knew that other people's need to say good-bye in a long ceremony with a body and a casket was not mine. Mother and I had been saying a slow, agonizing good-bye every single day for the last year.

I moved through the whole thing as if I was hosting a cocktail party, greeting guests, asking after their immediate comfort, wondering about the well-being of their parents and their kids. I was so goddamn charming. The Girlfriends were the only ones who really knew that if it had been up to me, I'd have turned off the lights and rolled myself in down comforters, even though it was the first of August, and hung out a sign: "Gone Fishing."

Not much got through to me, thanks to their shield. Every time they saw someone cornering me, one of them would whisk me away to a safe spot.

One busybody did get through. "Why didn't you bring those precious children? Don't you think they wanted to say good-bye to your mother?"

I had thought about how I would answer this. On an ordinary day, I would have looked long and hard at her before saying that I didn't want her hugging their tiny heads between her enormous, sagging bosoms and crying out to the Lord on their behalf. I didn't want people pinching their little cheeks in the name of grief. I didn't want people telling them scary stories about heaven and hell and death and sleeping into eternity.

I didn't want to have to explain to a two-year-old why the place Grandma went is so much better than where he lives, but why he can't go there now. I couldn't swear that there wouldn't be any family hysterics and I didn't want them to witness any. Funerals and crazy folks are synonymous.

I didn't say it though. Such a good girl. A good daughter. I nodded and tried to look grateful for her interest. "They're with Darnay's sister at his folks' house. They have been through a lot these past couple of days. They just weren't up to it."

Somehow, with Darnay and the Girlfriends' help, I got through the memorial service and the dinner after. I put myself in another place and another time to move through it. I thought that it wasn't so bad. I had lived through worse.

FORTY-THREE

We went back to Lansing right after the memorial service. I wanted to get home and figure out what it was like to move in the world as a motherless daughter, an orphan. And most important, most dreaded, I needed to get it over with—I needed to go home and face the empty nest. I was looking forward to trying to rebuild my life as Mother had wanted.

I thought I could do it seamlessly. The "funeral with no body" was supposed to be my last official act as the handmaiden of death. Once the memorial service was over, and I'd written the last thank-you note, all dues were stamped "Paid in Full." There would be no propping up of any leftover relatives. I wasn't asking anybody for critiques or for forgiveness for not burying her like they thought normal black folks ought to. I had no intention of listening to anybody's grief-stricken histrionics. Everyone was on notice that I wouldn't stand for a moment of bickering. It was done. Or so I thought.

The phone rang a week later, summoning me to the funeral home in Lansing. "We have a package for you," the caller said.

It must have been some rings and jewelry the hospice nurse had forgotten to take off. Or, maybe Mother said, "Stop, I'm still alive," seconds before they put her in that big gingerbread oven they use to cremate people. I'd go there and find her alive and whole, stuffing her jaws with her favorite chocolate-covered maple clusters, sipping a cola, waiting for me to take her home.

A little muddy-brown woman, with thick glasses, whose gloomy looks must have kept her from being employed anywhere but a mortuary, asked me to have a seat. I waited like a good girl, hoping that if I was really good, they would give me my mamma back.

As kids, we were told to hold your breath around dead bodies. Because if you didn't death might just fly up your nose and kill you too. Funny the things you remember and take to heart at times like this.

I held my breath until I got light-headed, then opted to breath lightly through my mouth instead of my nose. I looked around with ears perked, listening carefully for my surprise. I could probably hear her laughing with the undertaker, thanking him for sparing her. But there were no sounds—just me panting, trying to get enough air.

Finally, the undertaker came out and shook my hand. He cupped it in both of his, the way he was probably trained to do in mortuary school. They were warmer than I'd expected. I bet they taught him to warm his hands first. I started holding my breath again. He led me into his office, where I looked around for my mother, but she wasn't there.

"Here, we need to get these papers signed and then you can take her," he said, handing me a fountain pen. She was there, somewhere. He'd just said so. And I could feel her presence. She must have been in the back getting dressed, putting on her makeup, or having a bite to eat. I smiled at him, grateful, racing through the signatures without reading anything. It didn't matter. I was getting my mother back.

She was coming home with me, and this time I would get it right. I'd get better doctors, I'd make sure she ate and didn't waste away. I'd find some promising clinical trial that would let her in. I'd find experimental treatments. I'd find an herbalist. We'd eat special diets. If I hadn't been good enough before, this time I would be better. I'd keep her alive this time.

After I signed the last paper, the undertaker handed me the black metal box that sat on his desk.

"What the hell is this?" I asked.

"It's your mother," he said, as if there was nothing or nobody else it could be.

"No, this is a mistake." I really didn't understand. "No."

"You can purchase a nice urn to take with you, if that's what you mean," he said. "We are required by law to turn over the remains to you this way."

That wasn't what I meant at all. I studied the box in my hands, rubbing my fingers over it. Indeed, it had a label, "Earline Comer Terry," neatly hand-printed on it, with the date of her death and the date and time of cremation. I put it down.

"Thank you, but I don't want it. Do what you want with it." I turned to leave, not wanting to cry in front of him. Nobody had told me that when it was over, they give you a little box. Here sits the consolation prize. This is all you get in trade for a life. They give you a box with ashes as a token, a little something to remind you every day that your mother is gone and is not coming back. They should warn you.

"You don't understand, the law requires that we give them to you. You signed papers saying that you've received them."

I asked him what I was supposed to do with it. In movies they sprinkle ashes over the Pacific, or in English tea gardens, or over the bonny cliffs of Dover. But what does a black girl living in Lansing, Michigan, do? A few years back, I ran into an old friend of my grandmother at a restaurant, having dinner alone. She called me over and reintroduced me to Matthew, her late husband, who was housed in an ornate urn, sitting in the chair across from her, a martini in front of him.

After much useless debate, I left with a box, but it wasn't my mother. It was chemo, and nausea, and morphine. I could almost hear it scream out in pain. A Pandora's box, indeed.

When I'd driven into the funeral-home parking lot, I had worked myself into this frenzy of believing that Mother was somehow still alive. Less than an hour later, I sat in the parking lot looking at my passenger in a box. For the first time, I gave in to the disappointment and the sadness that had been building up over the past year. I sat in the car and wept in a way that I couldn't when I was the caregiver, or the funeral arranger, or the daughter who was being scrutinized by my relatives, or the mother who had to explain real death to her kids.

I pulled myself together and called my friend Beth, who had been through this with her father years before.

"I'm sitting in the car with a box that they say is my mother. What the hell do I do with it?" I asked.

"Open it," she said. "Don't you want to know what's inside? I did."

Opening it was clearly not an option. "Well, why don't you just tell me? There can't be that much difference in the ashes of a seventy-five-year-old Jewish man and a sixty-year-old black woman."

She proceeded to go into great and careful detail. "It's gritty, but not like cigarette ashes, more like charcoal ashes and little bits of bone," she said. "It's really pretty interesting when you think about it. It helps you realize that what's in the box isn't her. It's just stuff. Ashes to ashes crap."

I believed her enough to shake off any curiosity I might have had. I took a deep breath and drove like hell to my mother's apartment, where John was packing up the last of his things, getting ready to drive back to Gary, where he was going to live.

I handed him the box. "Here."

"What is it?" he asked, half-smiling, thinking it was a good-bye present. Maybe cookies for the four-hour drive? I looked in his eyes and saw the exact second that he remembered the gift was from me. His smile faded fast.

"They're her ashes. I thought you would want them," I said, knowing he didn't.

I turned to leave before he could protest too much or chase me down the stairs. I heard a thud, and turned to see the box on the floor, John staring at his hands as if they had been burned by hot coals.

I picked up the box, contents intact, and set it on top of one of the packing crates with a final force that said the box had found its home. Case closed.

"Why are you trying to give it to me?" he asked. Little beads of sweat had sprouted on his face.

"Because," I said, "she would probably like to have her ashes put with her mother, don't you think?" I was slow and calm on the outside, but shaking on the inside. "You're going to do it. This is not up for debate."

Waving my hand to signal that the conversation was over, I turned again to leave.

"You insisted on taking care of everything else. Why can't you take care of this?" he said. "You forget. I lost my wife. I can't drive all the way back home with her in the car, like this."

"You can," I said. "You will."

His tone changed from fumbling to adamant, with arms folded across his belly, as if he had found some new leverage against me. "I'm not doing it."

On the drive over, I'd wondered what I would do if he refused to take it. Then it came to me, or, I should say, she came to me.

My voice changed to that clipped, deliberate tone that Mother used when she was about to cut you off at the knees so cleanly that you didn't know you didn't have knees until three days later.

"Oh, you will. And I'll tell you why." I couldn't believe that I was saying it, but it felt good, so I just went with the flow.

He looked at me in such wide-eyed horror and fear that I could only guess that he was sure he was hearing her voice instead of mine. Maybe he was, because I am not usually so directly confrontational (I am much more likely to put a contract out on you than to do the job myself).

My mother had this habit of narrowing her large eyes into slits, making you think that she could see right through you to every secret you kept from her. And when she was on a real roll, her head would shake back and forth with the beat of the words she was using to rip you apart. A lot of black women do the head thing. I threw those in for good measure, knowing that if I could make myself look just enough like her to make him think that she had stepped out of the great beyond, he would take the box, or jump out the window. His choice didn't matter one way or the other to me.

"And if you don't do this one little thing for her, I will take that box and march it down to the Dumpster at the end of the parking lot, and toss it in." Which I would never have done, but I pride myself on being a hell of a bluffer—that's in my genes too.

"You wouldn't . . ." He was stammering again, so flustered that he called me by her name. "Earl . . ."

"Then I will get in my car and drive to my house, where I'll pick up my phone and call Grandpa and her sister, her brother, and all her friends and tell them how I watched hysterically as you threw her poor, suffering remains in the garbage and said, 'Good riddance.' Who do you think they would believe?" I was a cross between my mother in rare form and Linda Blair in *The Exorcist.* He looked at me as if my head was about to spin around like a top.

"You are hateful. You always were a hateful little—"

I smiled one of my mother's best smiles. "You have no choice here. If I make that call, you might as well move to Coldass, Alaska. That little Dumpster story will follow you all over Gary like skunk cabbage. You will be your own little self-contained leper colony." I was getting exhausted. This channeling of my mother was draining.

"Do we have a deal?" I asked.

"This is not right. I've been through so much, but okay."

I extended my hand to shake on the deal, and then snatched it back. "Have a nice life." I waved and walked away—picking up speed. I was still worried that he might chase me down the hall and to the car with the box.

I never saw him again. But he did call a few days later to tell me that he had done the deed. He would have preferred to never talk to me again, but he probably felt that he had better complete his deal with the devil first.

"Exactly *what* did you do?" I asked.

"I took it to the cemetery. I found the spot where your grandmother is buried. I took a shovel and I dug a hole for the box."

"Geeeeez, you did what?" The idea that someone would see him out there digging a hole for my mother was a bit too much for me.

"Did anybody see you out there, making like Gravedigger Jones?" I asked.

I didn't need to know. I didn't need to think about him out there digging up daisies. I didn't need to think about what happened to the box once it left my possession. The idea of my mother lying someplace, cold, getting rained on, or stepped on, or waiting for me to visit her (which I have never done) is still more than I can bear.

Some people find comfort in knowing they can go out with a picnic lunch and a bouquet of flowers and have long chats with their loved ones. Not me. I like to think of those I love as live energy around me. Sometimes I can smell Estée Lauder's Youth Dew perfume, and know that my grandmother's presence is close by. When I get the strongest craving for an icy, cold Pepsi, I know that my mother is close at hand. There are times when I feel like the loneliest little orphan girl since Annie, and I swear that I can feel their arms around me, and I fall asleep. These images are better for me than a cemetery, no matter how many views there are of a babbling brook or lovely weeping willows.

EPILOGUE: TEN YEARS LATER

I've been a good, sturdy soldier for the most part. I have had no choice. You can't be of service to your husband and kids when you're in the fetal position. Having suffered through spurts of depression in my life, I am keenly aware of how seductive grief is. It's a comforting thing. I've been at the point where the only safe place is the bed, or the closet, or the bathroom. I know what it's like to cry every time a breeze hits you. I have been there and it's nearly impossible to get back.

I work at it every day, but it's like riding a wild bull. It bucks, you buck back. It tries to bounce you off, but you hang on.

Eight months after my mother died, my grandfather went into the hospital for a routine angioplasty, as if an eighty-six-year-old man can have a routine heart procedure. He sat up on the operating table, called out, "Lucille," my grandmother's name, smiled, and died. That was it. His heart got tired from the weight of living with loss. When relatives called with the news, I sighed. I was too numb to say anything but, "Oh. I'm the lone ranger now."

In some ways, it's easy to bypass the grief. For the first few years, I couldn't even get to the point of acknowledging loss.

Even now, ten years later, although I feel like I am getting better, I am still trying so hard to recuperate from witnessing her suffering that I haven't been able to focus on the emptiness that her death has left me with.

I still see tubes and ports, catheters and pain patches. I close my eyes sometimes and hear whimpering and crying. I see wasting away. Eyes beg me to help her, but I don't have that kind of power, and the help is so limited.

About a year after my mother died, I was on the treadmill, listening to a Sounds of Blackness song that I'd heard a thousand times, "A Mother's Love." But this time I heard something, a note, a word, a moan that knocked me to my knees. I wept and sobbed as if it were the day that she died. Darnay and the kids heard the commotion, and came barreling down the stairs to find me howling and crying and gripping the side rail of the treadmill.

The kids were scared. Their tightly wrapped, stoic mother rarely had anything resembling a tantrum except in response to some misdeed of their own. From the way they looked at each other, it was clear that they thought I was one phone call away from being whisked off in a straitjacket.

Darnay understood that this was the crash landing he had predicted for months. He pried my hands loose from the rails and held me until I spent myself down into nothing.

Another time, I was living large, shopping in Los Angeles. I had left the Beverly Center with an armful of bags and headed across the street to Loehmann's. My mother and Katherine had introduced me to Loehmann's in Downer's Grove, Illinois, when I was a teenager. Over my adult life, "couture dressing at a discount price" was our mother-daughter ritual. I never missed a chance to hit one.

So there I was. I moved from the silk blouses to the Italian wool gabardine pants, to the "back room," where they keep the really good stuff—the Anne Klein, the French imports, the real Donna Karan. I found an exquisite navy wool dinner suit, with hand-sewn detailing that would have made you cry. I looked at the tag, $800, and did a double take.

A woman came up in a black sweat suit. It wasn't one of the silky pastel ones that my mother was so fond of, but was more like the well-worn, nubby-in-the-thighs sweats that I wear when I'm not in L.A. in a flowered sundress, mules, full makeup, and sunglasses, pretending I'm a movie star.

She looked like I hope I do when I hit my sixties, if I'm lucky. She wore no makeup and there were little strands of gray showing from under her baseball cap. I smiled because I thought that she seemed to be a woman who was comfortable with herself. My mother and grandmother would tsk tsk her. They thought that once you hit thirty, you should never be seen outside your backyard without being in full armor.

I peeked over the racks at her as she manhandled my dinner suit. She said to the lady who was shopping with her, "I'm not paying eight hundred dollars for a suit in Loehmann's."

Her voice got my attention. It sounded familiar, comfortable. I knew this woman but I didn't know how I knew her. Her voice was soft and purring, but not affected. It sounded like whiskey and honey. She went on her way, and I headed off to the dressing room and started trying on clothes when the lightbulb of recognition went on. It was Nancy Wilson. I thought, "My God, I'm in Loehmann's, my mother's favorite store of all time, shopping with her favorite singer. I ran to put my pants back on so I could grab Nancy by the arm and drag her to the pay phone. "Ma," I'd say, "guess who I saw today."

I was going to get her autograph. I thought that I should buy the dinner suit because Mother would be impressed that I paid way too much money at Loehmann's for a suit that Sweet Nancy had looked at. Then I remembered that there was nobody to call, and that even if I bought the suit, it would be too painful to wear it.

ॐ

Ten years later, I live in the same house with the man my mother had entrusted with my care. My children are older, more assertive, and consume way more groceries. But everything else broke apart when my mother died and left me to figure out how to be a grown-up. The San Andreas Fault line is just starting to settle.

Every couple of weeks, I have a migraine that I swear is undiagnosed, metastasized brain cancer. Every time I go to Dana Watt, my wonderful nurse practitioner, I expect the worst, then I'm mad when she tells me I'm fine. I've become fanatical about early detection, even though I am ever aware that in the ten years since my mother died there still is no reliable diagnostic test that can identify this cancer at its earliest stages.

The CA125 blood test detects cancer markers in the blood, but it's unreliable. I sign up for all the cancer registries. They promise that they will call me or E-mail me when they get that big breakthrough. Sometimes I see myself at death's door, being taken over by an ovarian tumor the size of a Swiss exercise ball when a call comes from a stranger. "Mrs. Collier, we wanted to let you know that we have a new, reliable test for early detection. You should come in right away." I spend a lot of time thinking about what one says in such circumstances.

I am quite the little fatalist about this cancer that I am sure is out there in the bushes waiting to get me, but I do what I can. I have my annual Pap and pelvic exams, even though I know that ovarian cancer usually cannot be detected this way. A pelvic exam, where they stick their whole arm up you, as if you are going to birth a calf, can detect an abnormally enlarged ovary, but when it's that big, you already have a real problem. I do it anyway because I know I am supposed to, and who knows? I might not get ovarian cancer. It could be cervical or uterine.

So my last ditch-effort is the ultrasound. I slosh in every year, forty-five minutes after drinking a gallon of water, to submit to a pelvic ultrasound that takes pictures of my ovaries from all angles. *Smile for the camera, girls.*

I watch the technician as she types and measures and moves the equipment, looking for an affirming smile or a concerned frown. But she has been taught to have a poker face. Every year it comes back clean. They give me a count of my fibroids and tell me if they have grown, and send me on my way to listen to the time bomb by myself for another year.

It just gets worse, this time bomb. Shortly after my mother's death, I found out that my grandmother's sister, Aunt Em, had also died of ovarian cancer. That little tidbit jacked up my risk factors. When the actor Pierce Brosnan's wife, Cassandra, died of ovarian cancer, I cried for her like I had lost a sister. Next came the actresses Sandy Dennis, Jessica Tandy, Colleen Dewhurst. I took all of their deaths personally, as muse callings, whispered warnings: *It will get you too.* They were two-minute warnings for this hereditary time bomb. It started ticking so loudly in me that I could hardly hear myself think.

Then I found a cancer hero in magazine editor Liz Tilberis. She was beating the ovarian cancer beast with a giant can of whoopass. She was making a difference to people who needed to see someone doing well. I became obsessed with her comings and goings in the social columns of the fashion magazines. Her book *No Time to Die* replaced Gilda's as my favorite reading because Liz lived to tell the story. If she lived, then there would be hope for me if I got this disease. Then I picked up *USA Today* one day and read that Liz Tilberis had died too.

My reaction was to make an emergency appointment with Dana, as I did every time I heard about someone dying of ovarian cancer, as if the cancer bug could be passed through the wind or through headlines, directly to me.

St. Dana was used to me by then. She knew that I thought of myself as Dead Woman Walking. She never got upset when I called because I found a mole, or when I swore that my abdomen was distended, or when some wife of a college basketball coach died of ovarian cancer. She just said, "Come on in. We'll take a look."

I read everything. I subscribed to really odd medical journals, and came marching in with a million questions. She smiled patiently and nodded, although she always sounded like I made her weary.

I developed an odd habit. I started sleeping with both my hands cradling my lower abdomen, and due to the effects of gravity, two children, and weight gain, I had plenty to cradle. I was sure that I was holding it because it was channeling some secret message about an upcoming cancer, but a psychologist told me that I was cradling it to try to protect it from illness.

She also explained why I hadn't lost the twenty pounds I'd gained while I was caring for Mother. I had resigned myself to the fact that I was a good cook and liked food, but she said that I was protecting myself from the inevitable.

"You saw her lose weight so fast. You ate to keep her alive. You watched her waste away," she said. "Now that you are so worried about getting the same thing, you are bracing yourself, giving yourself a reserve. A cushion."

At first I thought it was stupid. Why would anyone choose to keep on extra weight? Then I thought about how shocked I was anytime I ran into people who were sick with cancer or AIDS, how it frightened me to see their eyes sunken in and their behinds melted away. But this rationale gave me a get-out-of-jail-free card. I started to eat hell off hinges, and gained another ten pounds.

I was also lump obsessed. I read that there is a link between the genes that cause breast cancer and ovarian cancer. So I concentrated on my breasts—daily. I prayed that if I had to get a cancer, and I was sure that I would, it would be breast cancer. I was comforted knowing that the survival rate is higher with early detection. But I do love my breasts and I would hate to see them go.

I have been as ritualistic about getting a mammogram as I have been about the annual pelvic. It has been a rite of spring. One year not long ago, I had a mammogram that required a callback. I got the call on a Friday, which left me to stew over the weekend. *This is it. I just know.* The time bomb was ticking so loudly that I couldn't hear the kids screaming at each other.

When the call on the shadowy mammogram came, I called Dana, frantic. She sighed, calmed me down, and referred me to a surgeon to talk about exploratory options. "It's probably nothing, though," she said.

$\mathcal{3}$

I ended up with the surgeon with the beautiful hands. My mother's surgeon. "By looking at the mammogram, it seems that this thing, whatever it is, is too deep for me to be able to get at it with a simple needle biopsy here in the office."

"So what do we do?"

"We can set up an appointment to do a surgical biopsy under general anesthesia, or we can wait. Monitor it for six months. It doesn't look like anything to be concerned about."

He didn't know me at all. Everything was something to be concerned about. A part of me wanted to believe him. A part of me wanted to be relieved—to get my purse and my lumpy breasts and ride off into the sunset. But another part has always watched too much television and I thought of Julia Sugarbaker in an episode of *Designing Women,* in which one of Julia's friends has just died of breast cancer. The woman's doctor had told her to wait. In the meantime, Charlene has found a lump and is afraid to explore her options. Julia goes to the doctor with her and goes crazy when the doctor tells Charlene to wait. Julia's clipped, razor-edged voice is not unlike my mother's as she whispers, "This doctor is not the one who has to do the waiting, or do the dying if he's wrong."

Okay, Julia. Okay, Mother, I hear you. So I looked at him and his beautiful hands and I said, "If it was your wife or daughter, what would you have *her* do?" I shocked myself.

He shocked me even more. He didn't miss a beat. He said, "I would get her in over at Michigan State to have a stereotactic mammogram right away." This state-of-the-art procedure is done with computers and needles and television cameras.

"Well, I'll have that, thank you," I said in my best Julia Sugarbaker voice. And that is exactly what I had done. Fortunately, there was no cancer.

The experience marked a new moment in my outlook. I became my own contractor, much in the way that I was the contractor for my mother's illness. I would not be patted on the head and sent away. I didn't have time to be sick. I started to keep a log, a Command Central just for me. I asked even more questions. It was just as I'd told my mother: You don't really prevent illness by ignoring it. You just lose your vote in the outcome because in most cases, early detection and aggressive treatment can save lives that would otherwise be lost to cancer. I'm guessing that no woman really wishes she found her cancer later.

So Dana and I struggled along. I came in one day because my breasts were tingly. She explained that I was having perimenopausal changes. I didn't really believe her, so I went home and read my latest issue of *MAMM,* the breast cancer magazine.

Frantic again, I called Dana. "I have inflammatory breast disease."

"Why do you think that?" I heard her sigh.

"Well, the latest issue of *MAMM*—"

"Here is a thought. Maybe you should start reading mysteries or romances or the classics. Maybe you read too many medical journals."

⌁

I was the Mommy now. There was nobody to ask for advice about hot flashes and night sweats. I wanted to pick up the phone and tell Mother what I did or what I got, but she wasn't anywhere I could reach her.

Then there were moments that were such painful reminders of my loss. I went to the safety-deposit box and found a note in her handwriting. I went through my jewelry case and found one of her rings, so I wore it for a few days. I rummaged through the drawer where I kept old pictures, Mother looking like Diana Ross when she was a Supreme, Mother looking like Tina Turner, in her sandy-blonde wig days. Mother preparing her first Thanksgiving turkey, the one she didn't know she had to thaw first. Mother fixing my veil minutes before I walked down the aisle. Mother and Chris blowing out birthday candles, her sixty and his two. Nicole bossing my mother around, and Mother with this goofy, love-struck grin.

Then I found the glasses my mother wore every day. They were big and round and oversized, as was the fashion in the late seventies. They were my grandmother's before she died, and my mother took to wearing them to keep her mother close to her. I put them on and walked over to the mirror. Maybe this would help me feel close to both of them, I thought, but I couldn't see a damn thing. In the end, I didn't really need them to keep her close, or to see the world in the smart, loving way that she taught me to, because she was, and will always be, still with me.

I had been telling myself that I was okay now. Healed. After all, it had been almost a decade. Then the phone rang.

"Andrea . . ." It's Leslie, my best friend from college.

I said, "Hi, how are you?" but I instantly knew she was doing terribly. Her husband of over twenty years had been battling cancer for a little less than a year. I had been calling and E-mailing and sending the latest information on clinical trials and new protocols.

"Ted died on Thursday," she said.

In 1980 Ted and I worked for the same company. And as female coworkers are in the habit of doing, I set him up with my best girlfriend from college. I might have kept him for myself, but I was in my "beautiful bad boy" phase and he was much too nice and normal for me.

I can still see him making his way through busy downtown D.C. with me to meet her for lunch.

"Tell me again, what does she look like?"

I pointed her out at the corner, waiting for us. And that was, as they say, all he wrote. "I'm going to marry her," he said. I rolled my eyes and shook my head. But he did.

We held ourselves together as she told me about his last few days. I heard myself in her voice. I recognized the squeezing out of every single syllable of every single word. She was tired. She was overwhelmed. She recounted the details of the surgeries. She told me about the protocols and the medical centers. I winced as she talked about bridge hospice, which is what you got instead of full hospice if you were in a clinical trial. Only people who were not on any kind of treatment for their cancer got full hospice.

Big, stinging tears rolled down my face. She was the first one of my old friends who was a widow. *Widowed.* We were just kids. And I could tell as she talked about the last year, fighting a cancer that was basically incurable from the start, that she had been on a roller coaster too.

We talked about her son. And I realized that I was fortunate to have been thirty-six years old when the world turned upside down and not fourteen. I tried to imagine how his father's death would affect a fourteen-year-old boy, and my heart broke all over again.

Her voice got lower and smaller the longer she talked, and I knew that she had just ended one journey. But the one that she was beginning might be even worse because it never ends.

I listened carefully as she talked about the pain patches, the delirium. I knew she was talking to me, but she was also playing it back in her mind—all that she'd been through. I couldn't help but think about what we'd gone through ten years before. When she said that Ted tried to make it down the stairs and got stuck, she didn't have to explain. I saw my mother walk halfway down the long hall to the bathroom and forget how to get there, and how to get back to the bed. Leslie said, "He fought hard."

I said, "Don't ever forget that he didn't fight alone. You fought too." We got weepy.

I said something stupid. "He doesn't have to suffer any-more." How many times over the next few days would she hear that? As soon as I said it, I wanted to slap my own dumb self. I felt my lips tighten. I noticed that I was twisting and pulling strands of my hair at the nape of my neck, pulling them out, leaving a spot. This scared me, and I moved on to peeling the polish off my fresh manicure like the skin off grapes.

I was pacing again. I circled from the foyer to the dining room, through to the breakfast room, on to the kitchen, stopping to lean against the refrigerator for just a moment. It was just like the old days, when I was angry and scared and felt hopeless.

For decades Dr. Elisabeth Kübler-Ross has taught the terminally ill how to understand dying. She divides grief into five stages: denial, anger, bargaining, depression, and acceptance. They are Kübler-Ross's road map. But there has been no clear road map for those of us who watched, who cared, who loved, and who lost. There was just on-the-job training. Who told us how to pick ourselves up off the floor and go on? Who told us that the only comfort cancer leaves you with is this stupid cliché: "At least she won't have to suffer." That, my dear, has been some cold, hairy-assed comfort. For a long time it was all I had to curl up with. There was no sense to be made of it. I was not going to lie to Leslie and tell her that some miracle meaning was down the road.

Ten years later, I still pick up the phone to tell my mother a silly joke or I buy her something that I couldn't afford to buy before. Sometimes, when I look at my daughter and her friends, I want to ask her if I too was certifiably crazy at sixteen. I want to show her that I really do clean up pretty good when I want to. But I can't.

I asked Leslie if she wanted me to come for the funeral. I was relieved that she said no because I am terrible at wakes and funerals and would have been a handicap to her. I suggested that I was much better at mixing a bathtub full of toxic, frozen strawberry daiquiris and sitting around laughing at the good times and cussing out cancer. We agreed that this skill would be needed in the months ahead.

I thought about Ted, somebody I've known most of my adult life, getting some fast-acting cancer. Then I went over and looked at Darnay, who was sound asleep on the couch. *"What's growing inside you that I can't see?"* I whispered. I thought about my own little time bomb, ticking so loudly some days that I could hardly hear myself think. For the first time, I realized that I was not just sad, or tired, or joyful for the times we have had with those we love. I was also angry. I wasn't angry with God. I was angry with cancer.

But the good news is that I feel a little more whole every day. There is help, but it comes to me in unexpected ways. Wonderful people, often strangers, share with me their painful, beautiful stories about people they have loved and lost and I tell them mine. Sometimes we cry, we nod, and, oddly enough, we feel better because we share experiences that are different, but ultimately the same. Through talking about it, I find out that it really is okay to be angry with cancer, and that everybody gets around to moving on in the best way they know how.

The trick is in not letting the anger turn into a crippling fear that keeps you from living and laughing and loving the ones who are still here. The goal is to learn to use anger and loss in positive ways, like being smarter about your own health and the health of those you care about, being kinder to people, and figuring out that you have to live every single day to its fullest.

Sometimes now, when I think about the lessons I've learned and the ways that I have grown, I took at the picture that sits front and center on the mantel, the black-and-white photo taken in 1957 of my mother as a young woman, a single mother, proudly holding her happy little baby girl on her lap, saying, "Smile for the mommy." I smile back at her because I know how far we came together and how far I've come alone since she died. I can smile because I know that no matter how much time passes, or what happens, she is still with me.

ABOUT THE AUTHOR

ANDREA KING COLLIER consults on many health care policy and health advocacy programs. She has been a writer and marketing and public relations specialist for twenty years. She and her husband have a son and a daughter, and live in Lansing, Michigan.